SCENERY TECHNIQUES
for Toy Trains

Peter H. Riddle

KALMBACH BOOKS

Kalmbach Books
21027 Crossroads Circle
Waukesha, Wisconsin 53186
www.Kalmbach.com/Books

Published in 2011
15 14 13 12 11   1 2 3 4 5

Manufactured In the United States of America

ISBN: 978-0-89024-765-5

Unless noted, photos were taken by the author.

Publisher's Cataloging-In-Publication Data

Riddle, Peter.
  Scenery techniques for toy trains / Peter H. Riddle.

    p. : col. ill. ; cm. -- (Classic toy trains books)

  ISBN: 978-0-89024-765-5

  1. Railroads--Models. 2. Railroads--Models--Design and construction.
I. Title.

TF197 .R544 2011
625.19

CONTENTS

Simple scenery

Ranging from lightweight foam insulation board to ready-made trees, my O gauge layout employs numerous contemporary materials and techniques that can be used to develop unique toy train scenery.

Model railroading can be a fine art, and as with any artistic endeavor, the best results often come from experimentation, trial and error, and just plain hard work. After more than five decades in the hobby, and having built over two dozen layouts in four different scales, I have encountered my share of problems. As the old adage states, necessity is the mother of invention, and I have developed a number of construction and scenery techniques that produce results quickly and easily. I hope you will find these ideas helpful. However, feel free to develop your own variations on any of the ideas in this book. There are many different approaches to building scenery, and the more you experiment, the more satisfaction you will derive from the hobby. Above all, have fun. That's what toy trains should be all about.

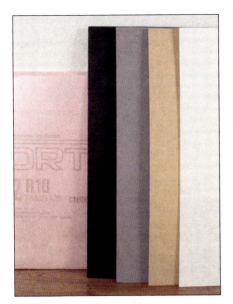

Rigid foam board (left) and foam core illustration board (right) are versatile and readily available products that can be used to initiate numerous scenery projects.

In addition to foam, polyurethane, rubber, and other flexible materials form useful scenery products, including the Pennsylvania Shale Cliff (left), the Palisades Sheer Wall (center), and tunnel portal components (right) available from Scenic Express.

Through years of experimentation, my quick and easy techniques have produced pleasing layout scenery, including this intriguing city scene.

In this book, I present ways to add scenery to a toy train layout that are simple to do and provide a layout with a satisfying appearance. These methods are aimed at taking a model railroad off a plywood tabletop and onto a base that facilitates building scenery with foam and other easy-to-use materials.

Creating scenery for a layout entails more than randomly adding some trees, mountains, and water. It includes adding streets and grade crossings, building structures, ballasting track, and making mini scenes. While this may sound like a lot of work and seem very realistic, it doesn't forget the fun of operating toy trains. I also show you how to incorporate animated accessories, build a geode mine, and feature a good ol' swimmin' hole.

Many of the techniques featured throughout the book make use of two versatile and readily available products: foam core illustration board and rigid foam insulation. The former is available from stationery stores, office supply stores, or art supply dealers, while the latter is sold by home supply stores.

Foam core illustration boards come in a variety of colors. The most useful colors for model railroads are black, gray, and white. Most have a white core, although the black variety can

also be obtained with a black core. This all-black version is useful for modeling asphalt streets. Illustration boards may also be used to build simple structures (Chapters 5 and 8) and used as a base for scenic plots (Chapters 4, 6, and 7). Common illustration board is ³⁄₁₆" thick and comes in various sizes such as 8 x 10, 11 x 17, and 20 x 30.

Rigid foam insulation board comes in 2' x 4' panels in thicknesses up to 2", and may be pink or blue in color. Although these boards are dense and essentially self-supporting, they are very lightweight. The pink and blue varieties should not, however, be con-

fused with commonly available sheets of white insulation, which are much less solid and prone to flaking. White foam panels are too flimsy for most modeling applications.

Along with foam, we'll use a variety of readily available commercial specialty products. Made from polyurethane, rubber, and similar materials, these products are molded into walls, tunnel portals, and other handy scenery elements. Available from hobby suppliers, these parts are easy to work with, and you can achieve satisfying scenic results in a relatively short time without any special skills.

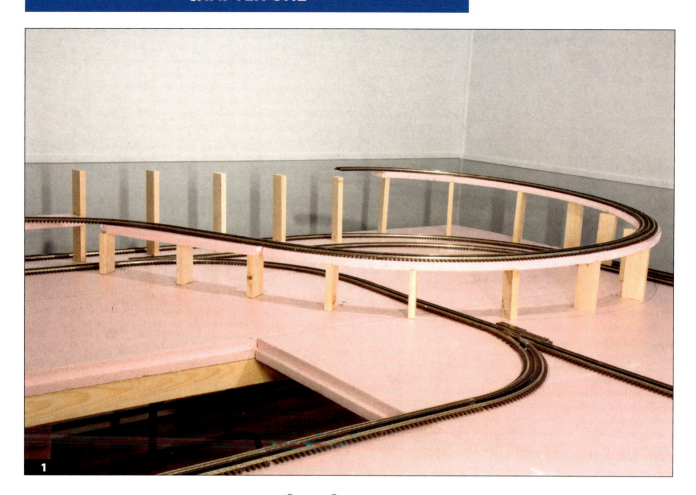

1

Foam tabletops and tracklaying

Think pink. Rigid pink or blue foam insulation board is a lightweight alternative to using plywood for layout construction and scenery.

Over the years, many excellent model railroads have been built on ¾" plywood surfaces. During that time, modelers have found it tricky to solve a number of problems in using this material. Plywood panels are heavy and hard for one person to handle, and they require a substantial framework to support them. It is difficult to build scenery that extends below grade, such as valleys and rivers, since the plywood must be cut out with a saw to place these features. And plywood has an unfortunate tendency to amplify sound, sometimes magnifying the rumble of the trains to an annoying degree.

Building a tabletop from rigid foam insulation boards is an alternate approach that anyone can do. Whether you are a beginner looking to build a small, attractive pike or a well-seasoned hobbyist with an established basement-filling railroad, you can enjoy satisfying results with creating a tabletop or scenery from foam, **1**.

Using foam insulation as a tabletop helps solve the problems inherent in plywood. The foam panels measure 2' x 8' and are very light—easily handled by one person. They come in varying thicknesses up to 2". At this thickness, the boards are nearly self-supporting, so a fairly lightweight framework is adequate for support. The panels are extremely easy to cut and shape, making below-grade features easy to accomplish. And best of all, they deaden unwanted noise effectively, allowing the sophisticated sound systems in modern toy trains to be heard to best advantage.

Choose either pink or blue foam board both for layout construction and for scenery, **2**. As mentioned in the introduction, avoid lighter weight white foam insulation, which is much less dense and also quite messy when cut. Small featherweight particles flake off easily, and the white boards have very little substance or rigidity.

Working with foam

The foam board panels may be fastened together as well as to a wooden table framework with foam board adhesive marketed especially for this purpose by hardware and building supply stores. For more on constructing train table framework, see one of Jeff Wilson's books on benchwork (Kalmbach Books).

Foam board adhesive is a form of contact cement. This type of glue works best when applied to both surfaces and allowed to dry until tacky, after which it will adhere to itself quite strongly. With an applicator gun, draw a bead of cement along the top edge of the wooden frame, **3**, and press the foam board in place on top of it. Immediately pull it apart again. Part of the adhesive will remain on the wood, and part will have transferred to the

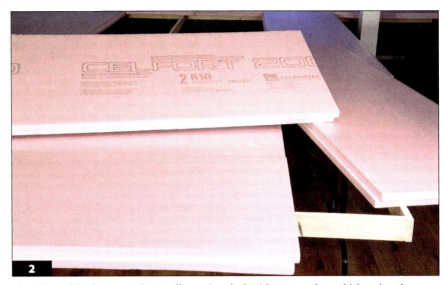

The edges of the foam panels are offset to interlock with one another, which makes them easy to fit together, especially when constructing a tabletop.

To apply the adhesive, draw a bead of cement along the wooden frame and then press the foam board in place on top of it. Then remove the foam board to spread the adhesive and reset it.

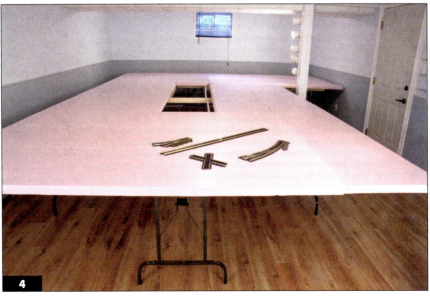

This photo shows the completed foam surface of my layout. A removable foam hatch will fill the open area at the center of the table.

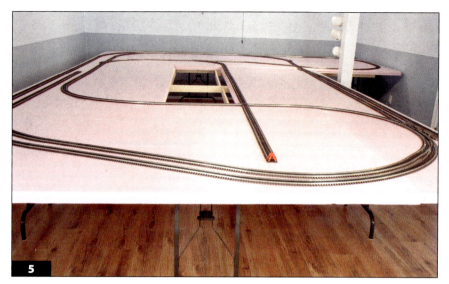

5 After assembling the foam tabletop, test-fit all track components to ensure that adequate space is available for track, accessories, and scenery.

6 Correct any issues in track alignment and then use a permanent marker to trace along the outer edges of each track section.

7 Wood risers of gradually increasing height can be used to build a grade between two levels of a layout. Space risers no farther than 10" apart.

foam. Allow it to air-dry for two to five minutes and then press the foam back in place. The adhesive will form a tight seal immediately, although it takes several hours to cure for maximum strength. Use the same technique when joining the edges of two foam panels together.

For ease of construction, try whenever possible to plan the dimensions of your layout to take advantage of the 2' x 8' size of the foam board panels. If you have to trim the panels, you can use a very thin-bladed knife and a metal straight edge or an electric hot foam cutter (detailed in Chapter 2).

Foam panels will support the weight of your trains and accessories easily but not the weight of someone crawling on them when adding scenery or making repairs. Therefore, on a large layout, you will need one or more access hatches to allow you to reach distant places, **4**. An access hatch made of foam board is very easy to lift out when necessary, as explained in Chapter 5. In general, the reach of an average adult's arm is about three feet, so no point on a layout should be farther away than that.

If your layout already has a table with a plywood surface, you can still make use of the advantages of foam. In fact, many of the scenery techniques we will be exploring depend on it. Simply glue foam panels directly on top of the plywood. You will then have an extremely rigid surface that is easy to work with, and one that will lessen the rumble of the train wheels.

Track planning

There are many excellent brands of track available to O gauge toy train operators today, ranging from traditional three-tie sections (familiar to Lionel train enthusiasts for more than a century) to more modern examples with integrated roadbed like MTH RealTrax and Lionel FasTrack. For a complete examination of the many products available, consult the book *Trackwork for Toy Trains* (Kalmbach Books, 2007.)

I chose Atlas brand track for this layout. It is a rugged product with solid steel rails mounted on dark brown plastic ties. Sections connect together by means of slip-on rail joiners. They come in many different diameters of curves, and in straight sections of varying lengths to suit virtually any track plan requirement. For those occasional situations where a ready-made section won't fit, Atlas also makes flexible lengths that can be bent to fit almost any situation.

I recommend that you assemble your entire layout and test it thoroughly before fastening the track down, to ensure that everything fits the space available and operates properly, **5**. It is much easier to make changes and adjustments at this stage of construction than when the accessories and scenery are already in place.

Connect your transformer and run your largest and smallest locomotives over all of the track while pulling a substantial load of cars. Correct any derailment problems, paying special attention to the alignment at switches and crossings. Be sure there is adequate clearance wherever you have a double-track main line. The geometry of Atlas track allows concentric curves to be installed with 4½" between the center rails of the tracks. Other brands vary. For example, most sizes of Ross Custom Switches curved track sections are designed to be installed 4" apart.

When the track plan is complete and tested to your satisfaction, outline everything with a felt tip marker and remove the track, **6**. This provides you with a guide as you wire the layout and fasten track.

Multilevel layouts

If you plan to build a two-level layout, you will have to construct a grade. A grade requires two components—a roadbed and wood risers to support it. Use foam for the roadbed and cut the risers out of 1" x 3" pine from a building supply store. The foam is flexible enough to conform to gradual changes of elevation but firm enough to support the track. It also helps the trains to run quietly.

Cut the foam roadbed a bit wider than the track—2½" is about right. Make the risers by cutting the pine boards in a miter box, and glue them

Use foam board adhesive to attach foam roadbed along the tops of the risers. Secure track to the foam using acrylic caulking compound.

Although the grade is partially hidden, this photo shows two levels of the layout with the track secured to the foam insulation board.

The addition of a scenic berm and the curved grade help disguise a steep climb between the two levels of the layout.

Lighting

Track lighting fixtures, mounted horizontally along the ceiling or to a vertical pole, can be used to highlight important scenes.

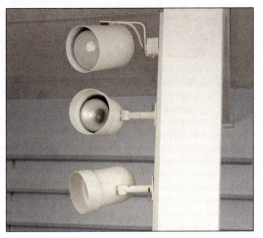

In fixtures using incandescent bulbs, try other colored bulbs to create interesting lighting effects.

Train layouts need plenty of light. You should have some sort of overhead fixtures, such as industrial-sized fluorescent tubes. If you have incandescent sockets instead, use floodlight bulbs instead of ordinary household bulbs to spread the light over a wider area.

You can also use track lighting with adjustable fixtures to draw attention to specific areas of the layout. The components are relatively inexpensive, and they require no special wiring expertise. The tracks can be mounted on any wooden surface with screws, or on drywall with wallboard anchors, and may be plugged into any electric receptacle. The light bulb fixtures snap into the track and are held in place by a rotating lever.

The fixtures in these photos are designed to hold 60- or 75-watt floodlight bulbs, which provide plenty of illumination. They can be tilted in almost any direction to show off whichever areas of the layout you wish to highlight. My basement layout room has two steel columns that support the overhead floor joists. I boxed them in with 2 x 6 pine and screwed the track lighting in place vertically, just above the level of the train table. That way they are within easy reach for adjustments. I plugged the unit into the main power bar so that the flood lights come on whenever the transformers are turned on.

to the layout base with foam board adhesive. Space the risers 10" apart, **7**. Grades should be no steeper than one-half inch for every 10 lateral inches of track, so each riser should be a maximum of one-half inch longer than the preceding one. A more gradual slope is desirable if you have enough space, both for easy operation and for a realistic appearance. At the beginning and end of the grade, there should also be an intermediate step of one-quarter inch per 10" section to ease the transition from level track to grade.

Next, glue the foam board roadbed to the tops of the risers using foam board adhesive, **8**. Attach the track on top of the roadbed with acrylic caulking compound. Curved grades are also easy to make with this method of construction, **1**. Assemble the track temporarily on the foam board, outline it with a felt tip marker, and cut along the lines with a thin-bladed knife or an electric hot foam cutter. Use foam board adhesive wherever two lengths of roadbed meet. It isn't necessary to put a riser directly under such joints. The foam is rigid enough to support itself over the 10" space between the risers, especially when the track is attached. You should avoid having a track joint and a roadbed joint at the same place, however.

Photo **9** shows some of the upper level of the layout in place. As you can see, most of the grade is hidden from view. Only a small part is visible, on the curve where it emerges from beneath the upper foam table top at the far end. This is desirable, because steep grades, especially when viewed directly from the side, are unrealistic. Curved grades tend to disguise this problem somewhat. (All of the risers will be concealed when the scenery is added later.)

Photo **10** is a view of that same area after the completion of the scenery. Notice how the curve tends to distract the eye from noticing how steep the grade is.

Hiding wiring

Before fastening the track to the foam, it may be easier to install and hide your wiring.

Any toy train layout must necessarily contain some compromises with reality, the most obvious of which is the presence of the third rail. But even more annoying to the eye are exposed wires, and especially those oversized lockons that accept the wires from the transformer.

You can eliminate this problem by soldering the wires to the underside of the track or to the rail joiners, **11**. If you are using GarGraves track, as shown in photo **11**, simply solder a short length of wire in the groove on the underside of each rail. If you are using Ross Custom Switches track, solder the wire to the flat bottom of

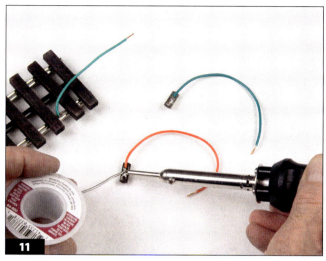

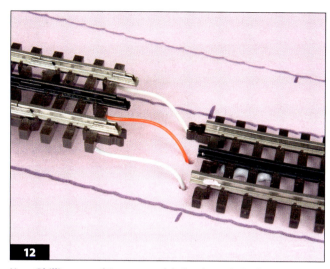

To avoid using unsightly lockons to connect power to the rail, simply solder short lengths of 18 gauge wire to the underside of the track or rail joiners.

Use a Phillips screwdriver to punch holes through the foam insulation board tabletop for hiding track wires. It's best to install track wiring prior to attaching any track sections.

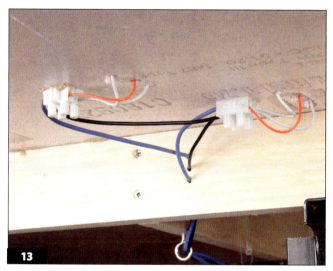

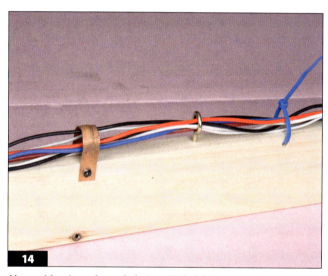

Connecting wires to miniature terminal blocks makes modifying or troubleshooting layout wiring a significantly more manageable task.

Along with using color-coded wires, it's helpful to organize and route layout wiring through cable clamps, screw-in hooks, or nylon cable ties.

the rails. Lionel FasTrack has its connections hidden under its integrated roadbed.

For Atlas track, solder the wires to the rail joiners instead, as shown at the center of photo **11**. Be sure that the wires are long enough to protrude through the table top and stick out beneath the layout when the track is installed. Three or four inches will be sufficient. Choose a different color for each rail to help you identify them when working beneath the layout. I use red for the middle (power) rail, white for outside ground rails, and green for any insulated outside rail that is used to control an automatic accessory such as a crossing gate.

Solder will not stick to the black coating on the middle rails or the middle rail joiners. Scrape the coating off with a file before applying heat. If your track has plastic ties, be careful not to touch them with the hot soldering iron, as they will melt and become distorted.

Only if the table top is plywood underneath the foam, do you have to drill holes wherever the wires pass from the track to the underside of the layout. This is another great advantage of an all-foam layout table. Set your drill aside. Simply poke round holes in the foam with a Phillips or Robertson (square) screwdriver. Feed the wires through the holes before you fasten the

track in place with the caulking compound, **12**. In this case, the red wire is the power wire to the middle rail, and both of the outer rails are grounded (white wires).

If you have a bunch of short wires sticking out on the underside of the table, you don't have to solder them all to longer wires in order to connect them to the control panel or transformer. It's no fun trying to manipulate a soldering iron above your head when sitting on the floor beneath the layout—especially if blobs of hot solder accidentally fall on your clothing or exposed skin. There is an easier way. Connect the wires together with miniature terminal blocks, **13**. These

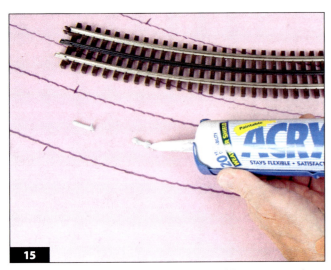

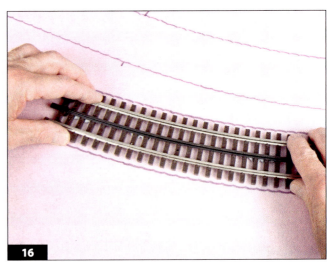

15 After transferring the layout design onto the tabletop, remove the track and apply short beads of acrylic caulking compound to secure the track sections.

16 Press the track sections into the beads of caulking compound. Use a wet rag to clean up any excess compound.

handy items are available at electronics supply stores in strips of eight or more, and are easily separated into smaller units with a razor saw. Attach them to the underside of the table with foam board adhesive.

In this application I used a blue power wire (middle rail) and a black ground wire to identify one of the throttles of the transformer. Route these wires from the terminal blocks to the control panel.

The underside of your layout shouldn't look like an explosion in a spaghetti factory, with wires running everywhere. When something stops working, it will take forever to find the problem. When that happens, you will want to be able to trace your wires quickly and easily. The best way to make this easier is to color-code all connections, and use different colors for each throttle of the transformer or transformers.

For example, assign blue and black wires respectively to the power and ground wires of throttle A on one ZW transformer. Use red and white for throttle B. If you have a second transformer, use yellow and black for A and brown and white for B. (Note that all ground connections are either black or white, while other colors are used for the middle power rails. You will want to be able to identify ground wires accurately wherever they are under the layout.) I strongly recommend that you write the key to your color code on a

file card and mount it on the back of your control panel for future reference.

Almost as important as color-coding is the proper organization and containment of the wires. You should run them along the wooden framework wherever possible. There are several ways to keep them neatly in place, **14**. At left in the photo is a simple copper cable clamp, which is screwed to the framework. At center the wires are threaded through a large screw-in eye, and at right I have drilled a hole in the wood and inserted a nylon cable tie. These ties come in a variety of sizes, and may be tightened to hold the wires firmly against the wood. All three of these items are available at hardware or building supply stores.

Fastening track

I chose not to install raised roadbed on this layout because the Atlas ties are thick and the rails are relatively high. I have found that once the ballast is in place, the track seems to be at a realistic height above the surrounding scenery.

Screws won't hold tight in the foam, so you'll have to try another approach. I recommend using acrylic caulking compound to attach the track components to the foam. You can use foam board adhesive instead (the same product with which you fastened the foam panels to the framework). However, that type of cement can be difficult to remove when dry. I rebuild

my layout frequently, sometimes as often as every two years, so I always try to recycle the table and reuse the track products. Therefore, I want to be able to lift the track quickly and easily without disfiguring it or damaging the table surface.

Acrylic caulking compound holds the track in place quite well, and it stays flexible and can be peeled off completely whenever you decide to make changes to the layout. In addition, it cures more slowly than the foam board adhesive, which allows you more time to reposition the track to correct any alignment problems. This product comes in tubes from hardware and building supply stores.

It isn't necessary to glue down every tie, **15**. Just run short beads of caulk down the middle of the outline you drew on the surface and press the track in place, **16**. Don't worry if some of the caulk ends up where it shouldn't. It cleans up quickly with soap and water, although after 12 hours, it will be completely waterproof. It is almost impossible to see the caulk between the ties once ballast is added, but you can use the gray variety, rather than white, because it will blend in with the ballast if any should happen to be visible.

After all of the track is laid down, all the wiring is in place, everything is tested, and it all works the way you want it to, you're ready to put in some scenery.

CHAPTER TWO

1

Foam scenery basics

In recent years, the use of rigid foam insulation to create model railroad scenery has begun to displace earlier methods, such as plaster, wire screening, and papier-mâché. The techniques involved in creating scenery, both above and below grade, out of foam insulation are simpler and considerably faster than these earlier methods, **1**. You can use foam insulation in all parts of the layout. The tabletop, flatlands, and mountains all can be made from this economical and easy-to-shape material.

Building a basic berm, hillside, or even a mountain peak, like the one shown here, becomes a much simpler project when using foam insulation board.

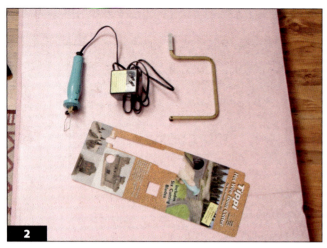

Although a knife blade or saw can be used to trim and shape foam board, a hot wire cutter is much easier and cleaner to use.

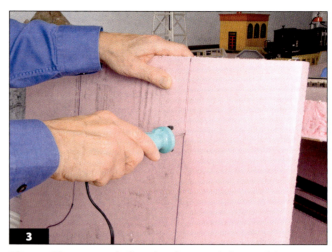

After marking cuts on the board surface, touch the tip of the cutter to the foam, activate the cutter, and allow the heat to melt the foam.

Avoid applying force to move the hot wire cutter through straight, curved, or beveled cuts. Always be sure to use the cutter in an area with adequate ventilation.

This 12" x 24" mountain stands 10" high. It is made from five stacked pieces of 2" foam insulation board.

Rigid foam insulation boards may be cut with a knife or even a saw, but the process is somewhat messy. Small particles of insulation will flake off, and because they weigh so little, they tend to get into everything. They're hard to sweep up, and static electricity makes them cling in all the wrong places. Fortunately, there's an easier way: a hot wire foam cutter. I use an inexpensive one called Tippi, available from Scenic Express (PC4774), 2. It comes with its own power transformer and a variety of thin wire foam-cutting blades. Operation is simple—just plug it in and push the button on the handle. In a few seconds, the wire blade becomes hot enough to melt its way through the foam board.

Making mountains

Use a felt tip marker to define your cutting line, 3. Touch the wire blade lightly to the foam, depress the button, and shortly it will begin to melt the foam. Proceed slowly, allowing the blade to do the work. Don't try to force the blade to move faster, as that will produce thin, wispy strings of melted foam.

A thin blade allows you to carve out almost any shape, such as the profile of a small hill, 4. Other blades can be used for scooping out depressions in the foam or carving details in the surface, such as rock formations. These and other techniques are described later in this chapter, and throughout the rest of the book.

In years gone by, modelers made mountains in several different ways. Some used wire screening covered with plaster, and some used papier-mâché. Another method involved making a basic shape from cardboard strips and covering it with plaster-soaked cloth or paper. These methods produced good results, but were messy and time consuming. All the work had to be done directly on the layout, often in hard-to-reach places. In addition, the finished scenery couldn't be easily saved or moved when rebuilding or changing a layout.

Rigid foam insulation solves all of these problems. It makes very lightweight scenic modules that can be constructed at the workbench instead of directly on the layout. By gluing layers

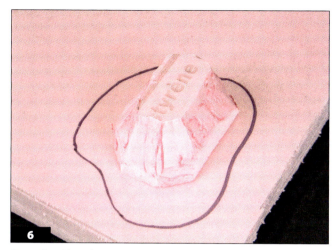

Carve the sides of the top section so that the base is wider than the top. Place this section on the next layer of foam and draw a wider outline around it.

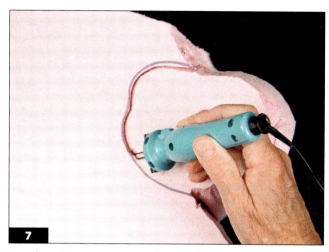

Use a hot wire cutter to cut out the second layer with a beveled edge. These rough cuts will be refined later, so don't worry if they don't follow the line precisely.

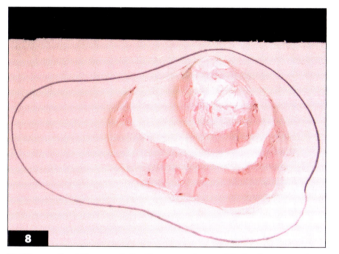

Outline and cut the remaining layers as done with the first two. The mountain should begin to look a bit like a tiered wedding cake.

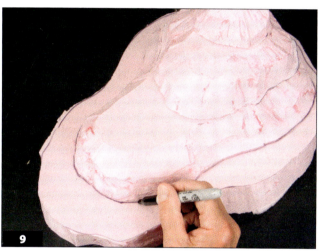

Stack the layers and trace the outline of the base of each one onto the layer directly beneath it.

of 2"-thick insulation boards on top of one another, you can build mountains whatever size your layout can accommodate. There is much less mess to clean up when you're finished, and it's easy to make changes later without disturbing adjacent areas of the railroad.

To build a hillside such as the one shown in photo **5**, first determine its approximate measurements, based on how much space is available on your layout. This one is 10" high, and occupies an area approximately 12" by 24". Make a simple sketch of the basic form and add any special features you want to include. I added a hiking trail that climbs in a spiral pattern from ground level to the peak.

For a hill 10" high, you will need five layers of 2" insulation. It's easiest

to begin this project with the topmost layers. Using a hot wire tool or a sharp kitchen knife with a thin blade, cut a rough block of foam a few inches wide. The sides should slant outward from the top toward the bottom, **6**. This will be the peak of the hill. Now set it on a larger piece of foam board and draw a rough outline of the next lower layer. The exact shape isn't important at this stage. All you need is a slab of foam that is the approximate size you want the hill to be at that level.

Cut out this new layer, again slanting the sides outward from top to bottom, **7**. It's best to use a narrow blade in the hot wire cutter. This is where you will begin to appreciate the advantages of this clever tool, which makes it much easier to achieve a more

rounded shape than you can manage with a knife.

Draw the next layer in the same manner and cut it out, **8**. If your hill is to be asymmetrical, like the one shown, make one side longer than the other.

Stack the layers and draw the outline of the base of each one on the top of the layer directly beneath it, **9**. This line is your guide for shaping the layers to fit. Note that the upper three layers in the photo have already been shaped with the hot wire tool. Follow the outline you have drawn and remove enough material from each layer, **10**, so they will blend together in a rough slope from top to bottom, **11**. It isn't important if the edges do not match up exactly at this point. The final shaping comes later.

Follow the outline marked on each layer and remove enough foam to make a more gradual transition between layers.

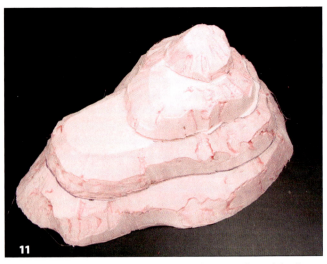

This photo shows the resulting transitions between four of the five layers of the 10" high mountain.

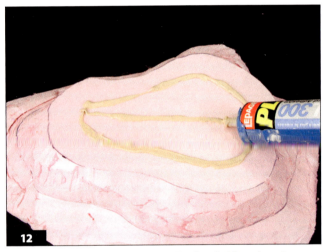

To bond the layers to each other, apply a bead of foam board adhesive in a circular pattern.

For a secure bond, press foam layers together and immediately pull them apart. After the glue becomes tacky, press them together again.

Bonding layers

The next step is to glue the layers together using foam board adhesive. You can use carpenter's glue instead, but it takes a very long time to dry because of the heat-retention characteristics of the foam. Foam board adhesive sets up fast and allows you to continue working within about five minutes.

There is no need to coat the entire surface. Just run a bead of cement in a circular pattern on one of the layers, **12**. Then press the adjoining layer against the glue. Immediately pull the layers apart, **13**, and allow the glue to dry for two to five minutes, until tacky. Then press the layers together again. The bond will be strong enough to hold while you continue with construction, but it may take several hours for it to reach maxi-

mum strength. After that, the layers will be almost impossible to separate.

Adding a trail

Photo **14** shows the completed contour of the hill, with all five layers cemented together. The next step is to refine the shape. For example, if you want to have a hiking trail leading from ground level to the top, begin by outlining the route with a felt tip marker, **15**. The path should have a relatively gentle angle of climb. Follow the line to carve out the path, using a knife or (preferably) a hot wire tool with a wide rectangular tip, **16**. Carve a horizontal groove about 2–3 scale feet wide (½" to ¾") in a spiral pattern from bottom to top.

Photo **17** shows the rough-cut, five-layer hill with the hiking trail that

encircles it, climbing from right to left. Note that on one side of the path the walls are somewhat steep, simulating a rock cut, as if the terrain had been deliberately shaped by the town's landscape department. If your mountain is located in a less developed area, you might want to avoid any suggestion of human intervention by making the trail more rugged as it follows the natural topography. This view also shows evidence of additional carving to further refine the overall shape.

When you are satisfied with the appearance of the hill, use a dull-bladed table knife to cover it with a thin layer of crack filler compound, **18**. This seals the foam and smooths out the rough edges left by the knife or hot wire tool. Pay close attention to filling the seams

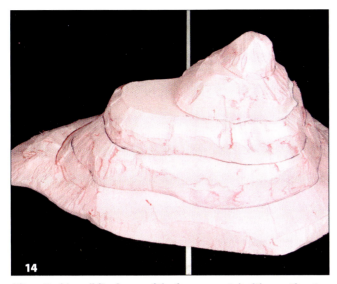

14

After attaching all five layers of the foam mountain, it's now time to apply details, including a hiking trail and various rock outcroppings.

15

Use a permanent marker to indicate where the hiking trail will travel from the lowest level up to the peak.

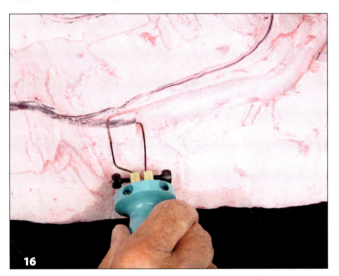

16

Use a hot wire cutter to carve an approximately ½"-wide groove that follows along the outlined path.

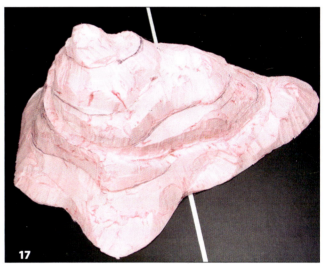

17

This photo shows the mountain with a hiking trail carved up and around the foam layers. It's now ready for additional details.

18

To seal the foam and smooth any rough edges, use a putty knife or table knife to cover the entire mountain with a thin layer of crack filler.

19

After the filler dries, cover the entire mountain with tan or brown textured wall paint. Add areas of gray to suggest rock outcroppings.

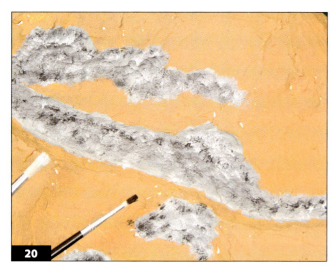

20

Add subtle variation and strata to the rock outcroppings by using a small paintbrush to apply other light and dark shades of gray paint.

21

While the paint is still wet, sprinkle fine gravel or ballast over the hiking trail, using a finger to press the loose material into the surface.

22

To give the mountain more texture and character, sprinkle green and brown ground foam material over the wet paint.

23

Allow the paint to dry overnight, invert the mountain over a trash can, and shake off any excess material. Now it is ready for final details.

where the layers meet. You will want to hide any evidence that the hill was constructed from uniform 2"-thick slabs.

Finishing the hill

Paint the entire hill with a base color such as tan or brown. Then use gray paint to suggest rocky areas, **19**. The most natural places for rock formations to occur are in vertical or steeply sloped areas, such as the cuts beside the path to the summit. I used a textured paint that contains rough sandy grains to simulate an uneven surface. For the most natural appearance, use several different shades of light and dark gray, **20**. (Because Nova Scotia soil contains a lot of limestone, I also added some patches of white.) A small paintbrush works best for these details.

To give your hikers a gravel surface to walk on, brush a thick coat of paint on the path, a small area at a time. Then sprinkle scale gravel or fine ballast over the path and press it firmly into the paint, **21**. Shake off the excess when the paint is dry. Adding such details is an enjoyable part of the project, during which you can give free rein to your artistic talents. Because you will be working at a bench rather than directly on the layout, cleanup is also relatively easy.

The next step is to add weeds, grass, and other foliage. I chose six different products from among the huge variety of colors and textures available from model railroad supply companies, **22**. Employ the same technique you used for putting gravel on the path. Spread paint thickly

wherever you want the foliage material to adhere, and sprinkle it on generously. When everything is dry, invert the mountain and shake it gently so any excess material will drop off, **23**.

Consider adding a few details to bring the scene to life, **1**. I found a few O gauge-size goats and mountain sheep in my scrap box, as well as a trio of intrepid rock climbers. You can also find scale-sized campers and hikers in your favorite hobby shop, in the catalogues of such companies as Arttista Accessories (www.arttista.com), or online.

Place your mountain on the layout, blend its base in with the surrounding scenery using crack filler, paint, and grass or weeds, and the project is complete. We'll tackle some vertical surface areas next.

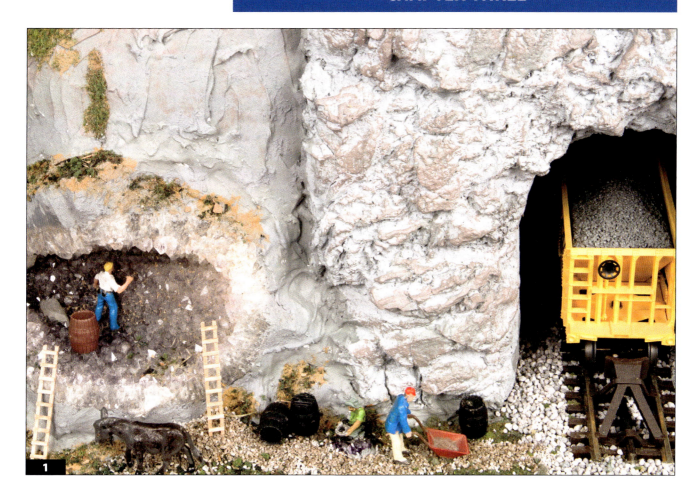

CHAPTER THREE

1

Scenery for vertical surfaces

Building a model railroad to represent the real world always involves compromises.

Unless you are fortunate enough to have a huge train room, running your train on

multiple levels is one way to extend your trains' operating environment. You will also

probably have to compress the scenery to a greater extent than would occur in na-

ture. One of the main problems encountered when building multilevel layouts is how

to disguise changes of elevation in a restricted space, **1**.

Disguising the vertical space between two levels of a train layout is a common challenge, which I solved here by adding a mining scene.

2

Another option for hiding vertical space is using a prefabricated rock formation to which I added three intrepid rock climbers.

On smaller layouts, there isn't enough room to put in gentle slopes, and there are a number of products on the market that will help make steep hillsides seem realistic. For example, you can buy preformed foam panels that represent various types of natural stone formations as well as masonry walls.

To fit a bilevel track plan into a small area, you will have to put up with some vertical or near-vertical walls. I blended a prefabricated polyurethane rock formation (Scenic Express MM0880) into the layout by attaching it to carved panels of foam insulation board, **2**. Prefab foam scenery products are lightweight, easy to reshape, and accept paint well. By adding some paint, ground cover material, a few bushes and trees, and figures from companies like Arttista Accessories (www.arttista.com) to these products, it is easy to create interesting scenes for your layout.

Theoretically, you could construct an entire layout with such products, although that would involve considerable expense. It is more economical to install them in conjunction with walls made from rigid foam insulation boards.

Blending in a tunnel portal

It is a simple process to blend a rock-faced tunnel portal (Scenic Express FL6550) into a hillside. Begin by fastening the portal in position with foam board adhesive and then glue on slabs of foam in the approximate shape of the surrounding scenery, in this case a steep hillside, **3**. To prevent the slabs from shifting or coming apart, be sure the cement has dried sufficiently before you start shaping the foam.

Don't worry about achieving a tight fit at this stage. All you need is a rough approximation of the eventual shape of the terrain. There may be gaps between the foam slabs and the tunnel portal,

but they will be filled in later. Shape the slabs by removing excess material with a hot wire foam cutter or a knife, **4** and **5**. You may have to bend the wire blades of the foam cutter to get into tight spaces or around corners. You needn't be too fussy at this stage of construction. Just work toward a general outline of the hillside or mountain.

Next, coat the foam with a layer of drywall compound, **6**. This product comes premixed in various quantities in plastic buckets and is more economical to use in large areas than the crack filler that we applied to the small hill in Chapter 2. It is also somewhat thicker and can be used to fill gaps between pieces of foam and prefabricated scenery items.

Apply the drywall compound with a flat-bladed table knife. Work it into the spaces between the foam board and the tunnel portal. Allow it to dry completely. Thin layers will cure overnight, but thicker areas may take several days.

3 This photo shows the initial step for integrating a rock-faced tunnel portal into a vertical area that also includes foam insulation board.

4 After installing pieces of 2" foam board around the portal, use a hot wire cutter to carve a gradually sloping face.

5 Use the same hot wire cutter or a thin-bladed knife to carve mostly horizontal rock strata into the foam board.

6 Cover all exposed surfaces of the hillside with drywall compound and fill the seams between the foam boards and the portal.

The only problem with drywall compound is its tendency to shrink somewhat as it dries, resulting in minor cracks in the surface. Fill these cracks with an extra application of the compound and let it dry completely. Don't rush this stage of construction, or you will have to make frequent repairs later.

When the drywall compound is completely cured, you can carve it to simulate a rock wall, layers of shale, or a simple dirt hillside, **7**. For ideas, you can look through the pages of magazines such as *Model Railroader* and *Classic Toy Trains* or consult the illustrations in the Scenic Express catalog. You could even take a ride in the country and observe your surroundings. Take photos of any formations that appeal to you. You can spend as few or as many hours as you wish working on these details. When the work is no longer satisfying or fun, move on.

All you need to do to finish the portal is paint it several shades of gray and brown, add some turf, and place ballast around the track, **8**. In this scene, the bumper at the end of the track is temporary. The layout will eventually be expanded from this point.

Being imaginative

Model railroading does not have to be 100 percent serious. Master modeler John Allen, whose Gorre & Daphetid empire often graced the pages of *Model Railroader* a few decades ago, gave his visitors many a chuckle with little surprises scattered around his pike. My favorite scene was a quarry where ponderous dinosaurs hauled wagonloads of gravel to the railhead. In the same spirit, why not liven up an empty corner of your layout with a not-quite-realistic scene, such as this one where miners are extracting something more exotic from the hillside than simple coal.

I started with a special rock that you can buy from a souvenir shop—a geode, **9**. A geode consists of a hollow igneous or sedimentary rock that contains crystals formed when minerals were deposited by groundwater. The crystals are revealed when the rock is broken open. Geodes may contain anything from plain clear quartz to sparkling semiprecious gems of many colors. The raw amethyst such as the one I used makes a perfect starting point for a fantasy mining operation. You will need a few workmen, such as those shown in the photo, to complete the scene. The little pewter miner sitting on his own chunk of amethyst also came from a local souvenir shop.

If your scenery is constructed from rigid foam insulation, it will be easy to sink the geode into the hillside. Just cut away the foam in the approximate shape of the outside of the rock, **10**. It's a messy job, leaving lots of small pieces

Allow the compound to dry thoroughly and then use a thin-bladed knife to carve out rock detail.

Complete this hillside project by covering the compound with earth-toned paint and adding various textures and colors of ground foam.

With a little imagination, a souvenir or thrift shop discovery, such as this geode, can become a complete mining scene.

Use a thin-bladed knife to carve away enough space to fit the geode into the hillside. Scrap pieces of foam help keep the geode in place.

of foam to clean up, but it doesn't take long. Support the geode with scrap pieces of foam placed underneath it, and glue everything in place with foam board adhesive.

Now seal the spaces between the hillside and the geode with crack filler or drywall compound, **11**. When it's dry, fill any cracks that may have developed because of shrinkage and then cover the area with latex paint to match the surrounding rock scenery, **12**. Add some brown paint to simulate areas of dirt, and while the paint is still wet, sprinkle on foliage to suggest weeds and natural debris.

Don't forget to make a path for the miniature workers to use in getting their product to the rail siding. Spread fine ballast between the mine and the tracks to represent gravel. You can spread the ballast over wet paint, as described in Chapter 2 or use matte medium to fasten it in place. This

useful adhesive is available in artist supply stores and from model railroad suppliers such as Scenic Express. It comes premixed or in powder form. You can spray it on or apply it with an eyedropper, **13**. It dries clear to become virtually invisible.

The miners are busy, one chiseling chunks of amethyst out of the walls, one cleaning and sorting the pieces, and another carting away waste in the wheelbarrow, **1**. I painted the little pewter figure and sank his small chunk of amethyst into the foam top of the layout around the corner from the mine entrance. This took just a couple of minutes to accomplish, but if the table had been made from plywood, the job would have been much tougher. The miner spends his time sorting and cleaning the gems that his coworkers carve out of the cave.

To complete the project, add a few details—for example, a couple of rustic

ladders, some kegs, a wheelbarrow, an ore car on the siding, and a mule to do the heavy work, **1**. Little scenes like this one add charm and interest to a layout, and also provide industries (even improbable ones such as this) to generate revenue for the railroad. All you need is some imagination and an hour or two of time.

Building retaining walls

Adding retaining walls is one way to heighten variety with terrain. Few of us are lucky enough to have sufficient model-sized real estate for extensive rolling countryside and gradual transitions from flatland to mountains. The limitations of available space on multilevel layouts often make it necessary to have very steep cliffs or hillsides, much more precipitous than are usually found in nature. A good way to disguise this problem is with retaining walls.

11 Seal the base of the geode and gaps around the perimeter with crack filler or drywall compound.

12 After allowing the compound to dry, paint the hillside and other new surfaces to blend with the original earth-tone colors.

13 To secure the fine ballast along the walking path, apply drops of diluted matte medium with an eyedropper.

14 To build retaining walls, first install the vertical pieces of foam board used to support prefabricated wall sections.

15 Prefabricated retaining wall sections come in a wide assortment of sizes and styles. I chose quarried stone walls and a tunnel portal.

16 Use a hot wire cutter to carve out rough chunks of foam from the hillside area above the retaining wall.

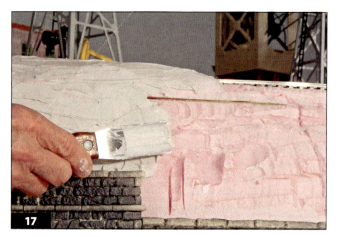

Coat the craggy hillside surfaces with drywall compound. Be sure to fill the gaps between the foam and retaining walls.

Cover the hillside with a base coat of gray latex wall paint, and add reddish brown highlights.

To simulate soil on the hillside, randomly apply several thick patches of brown paint.

While the paint is still wet, sprinkle fine turf and other ground foam materials to add texture to the hillside.

To build, start by installing vertical slabs of foam insulation between the upper and lower levels of the layout, **14**. As with the tunnel portal, you need to achieve only a rough approximation of the eventual terrain. I've used two different thicknesses of foam here, both 1" and 2". The thinner stock is useful for scenery but is less self-supporting. The foam serves as a backdrop to support the prefabricated retaining walls.

Next, add your chosen molded scenic products, **15**. I used a simulated quarried stone tunnel portal, a retaining wing at left, and retaining walls and gap fillers at right (all from Scenic Express: FL6262, FL6190, FL6150, and FL6158). The gap fillers are simulated stone projections that hide the joints between the retaining wall panels.

With a broad rectangular blade in the hot wire tool, carve the hillside into a rough approximation of rocky terrain, **16**. Dig deeply into the foam to create craggy outcroppings or crevasses.

Coat the surfaces of the foam with drywall compound, working it into the carved surfaces to highlight them, **17**. Be sure to fill the gaps between the foam and the retaining walls and tunnel portal. Allow the compound to dry thoroughly and fill in any cracks that appear when it shrinks.

Once the surface is carved to your satisfaction, apply an overall base coat of paint, **18**. I chose gray to emphasize the rocky nature of the landscape and then overlaid it with highlights of reddish brown (iron ore, perhaps?).

The next step is to plant some vegetation. You can purchase a huge variety of grass, turf, dirt, and rock materials from hobby suppliers, in colors appropriate to any season of the year. They come in fine, medium, and coarse textures and are made from various fibers such as ground

foam, rubber, lichen, and natural products.

Weeds will grow wherever soil is present, including in crevices and between rocks. To simulate this, dab some brown paint on the rock wall wherever it looks likely that some airborne seeds might take root, **19**. While the paint is still wet, sprinkle turf over it, **20**. It's best to use relatively thick layers of paint, as it dries quickly, and the turf material will soak it up.

On vertical surfaces, press the turf material into the paint with your fingertips, **21**. Don't attempt to hide all of the paint. Some dirt showing through between the weeds will look more natural. Add extra vegetation on horizontal surfaces, such as on top of the tunnel portal and the retaining wall.

Once the paint is completely dry, clean up the excess with a handheld vacuum cleaner, **22**. This is one of the most useful tools to have on hand when

21

Due to the steep pitch of the vertical surface, I used a light touch to press scenery materials into the wet paint.

22

Once the paint is dry, use a handheld vacuum cleaner to clear stray bits of scenery material from the tabletop.

23

A prefabricated sheer wall provides the perfect backdrop for a railroad trestle installation.

24

This completed canyon scene features foam-board rocks, a painted sheer rock wall, and a trestle made from precut components.

25

An instant hillside, like this one from Scenic Express, can provide a colorful scene in a fraction of the time it takes to build one.

26

Other prefabricated scenery components, like this Scenic Express shale cliff, are manufactured with exceptional detail.

Layout corners are often odd spaces that might benefit from additional scenery. This prefab installation, aptly named Deadman's Corner Unit, came from Scenic Express.

making scenery. Choose one with a narrow nozzle like the Euro-Pro model shown here, which can suck debris out of narrow cracks and crevices. If you start with a clean vacuum, when you empty it, you can save the material to use again.

Installing trestles

You can use a trestle, such as the wooden Grand Central Gems Bridge System from Scenic Express, to span gaps in upper-level scenery.

To look realistic, a trestle needs a natural background, such as the Palisades Sheer Wall (Scenic Express FL1002), which gives a good imitation of a canyon wall, **23**. Surround it with blocks of foam insulation to complete the terrain, shape them, and create texture with drywall compound. Depending on the height of your trestle, you may have to dig out a depression in the table to accommodate the longest legs. Then proceed with the final shaping of

the foam; do some painting; and add trees, vegetation, and other elements.

Photo **24** shows the same area of the layout after installation of the trestle. The gray and lighter brown colors added to the palisades rock formation and the green foliage afford a pleasing contrast to the wood tones of the trestle.

Saving time

Even if you can only spend a few hours each week working on your railroad, you can still get good results with prefabricated foam castings, which are great timesavers. For example, if you need an instant mountain, or simply don't want to take the time to make another one like the one featured in Chapter 2, you can buy Inspiration Point from Scenic Express (MM0860). Photo **25** shows this unit in place on an area of the layout under construction, where final detailing is still incomplete. A few trees are in place,

and the base of the casting is surrounded by heavy debris consisting of simulated weeds and dead branches. Mixtures such as this come ready to use from hobby supply companies.

Another useful prefab product is a shale cliff (Scenic Express FL1230), **26**. There is plenty of attractive detail already present, inherent in the textures and shadows of the surface. You can use such products "as is" or detail them with highlights of paint and vegetation.

If you build up the terrain in a corner, it tends to detract from the rectangular nature of the layout. You can construct a low simulated dirt or rock hill from rigid foam insulation board or buy a prefab version, such as Deadman's Corner Unit from Scenic Express (FL1003), **27**.

Next, we'll turn our attention to providing access to hard-to-reach areas of the layout. At the same time, we will create places for the residents of this miniature world to live.

CHAPTER FOUR

Sidewalks, houses, and hatches

A railroad without a miniature population is sterile, and the people need places to live and work and play. The center of a layout is often a good place to situate towns and cities, but it can be the hardest place to work on. It can be hard to reach the middle of a layout, and you never want to crawl around on top, even if it is sturdy enough to support you. Once the scenery is in place, no matter how careful you are, you are likely to dislodge or damage small details every time you have to repair something. Sooner or later, you will need to be able to reach every spot on the layout, **1.**

As a result of practical planning, I can easily reach this residential neighborhood and surrounding layout scenes by simply lifting up an inconspicuous foam access hatch that's hidden beneath the structures.

Lightweight foam insulation board is the key to building a concealed access hatch that's easy to remove yet rigid enough to support scenery and structures.

With minimal effort, you can lift the entire access hatch and rest it on another area of the layout, all without fear of damaging other scenes.

The concept for building scenes on panels originates from the Lionel Corporation's miniature houses mounted on individually landscaped boards.

On a quiet residential block, sandwiched between trolley tracks and a steep hillside, the citizens of a railroad town on my layout are attending an outdoor wedding at the local church, **1**. This settled neighborhood conceals a secret, one that is essential to the maintenance of any large model railroad. The streets, sidewalks, houses, cars, and people are all mounted on a rectangle of foam insulation board that can be lifted out whenever you need to work in this area.

Access hatches

While laying the track and completing the perimeter scenery, I left a 24"-wide clear space in the middle of the layout. This area is set on two foam insulation boards, carefully trimmed to drop into place with just a little clearance on all sides, **2**. I chose to create a simple residential area rather than an industrial district on these removable hatches in order to keep the weight down and to avoid the extra wiring that would be required by operating accessories. The only wiring the hatches need is a single feed for the lights in the houses.

Insulation panels make excellent lift-out access hatches. Even if the rest of the table is covered with plywood, consider using these lightweight removable panels wherever you need access when working on a hard-to-reach area on your layout. My layout features two access hatches that rest on top of the basic table framing and can be removed by simply popping them out and upward from below, **3**.

Houses don't look convincing without lawns, front walks, driveways, cars, and people. One great advantage of using rigid foam panels for these hatches is that you can detail them at your workbench, which is usually easier and faster than leaning over the layout.

Streets and sidewalks

To speed up the construction process, we'll borrow an idea developed by Joshua Lionel Cowen when he was searching for ways to persuade Lionel Trains customers to build their own layouts. He marketed miniature

5

Start building your neighborhood with sidewalks made from 1"-wide strips of gray illustration board. Use a pencil to apply expansion joints.

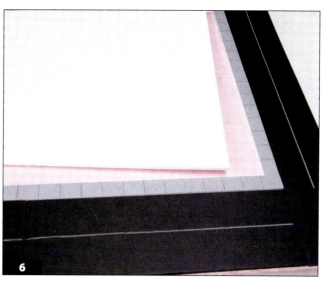

6

Make asphalt roads from black illustration board cut at least 5" wide. Yellow carpenter's glue will attach the roadway pieces to the hatch.

7

Assemble pieces of white illustration board over the hatch. Use this board to test-fit the arrangement of structures, roads, and sidewalks.

8

Use a pencil to lightly outline the structure placement and then cut out the areas where driveways and front walks will go.

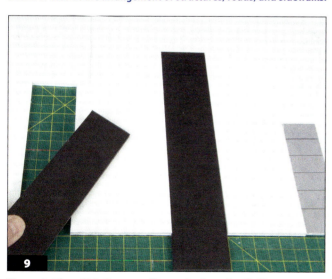

9

Now cut strips of black or gray illustration board to fit the spaces intended for driveways and front walks.

10

Build a foundation for each house using strips of balsa or basswood cut to fit inside the outline of each structure.

Form flower beds and lawns by adding brown paint to specified areas of a property. Next, sprinkle brown turf over the wet paint.

Press the turf firmly into the paint with a small wood block. After the paint dries, use a vacuum to remove the excess turf.

Add a lawn by painting areas around houses with a brownish gray paint. Avoid using the same shade of brown applied under the flower beds.

houses already mounted on individual landscaped boards, **4**. By making it easy to add residential neighborhoods to a railroad, Cowen hoped to create a greater demand for his products from youngsters and their parents who might be encouraged to keep their trains set up year round and not just at Christmas. In the same manner, you can quickly build a single scenic plot or an entire neighborhood on pieces of foam core illustration board. Using this product makes the job go quickly, and it is readily available from stationery stores, office supply stores, or art supply dealers.

First, you must design a pattern of streets, sidewalks, and lawns to accommodate your houses. One 4-foot access hatch will accommodate three O gauge-size houses in a short residential block. If you put the streets along the sides of the hatch, the straight edges will make it easy to align the hatch with the rest of the layout. Looking back at photo **1**, you'll see that it is very hard to see the edges of the hatch along the roadways. The edge is a little more visible at the back, where the well-cared-for lawns butt up against the meadow and trestle area. But as you can see in photo **17**, this is less obvious when you view the railroad from a lower, more natural angle.

It's easy to mass-produce sidewalks by cutting a series of 1"-wide strips of gray illustration board. Foam core illustration boards may be easily cut with a straight edge and a sharp No. 11 hobby knife blade. Using a pencil and a square, draw simulated concrete expansion joints at a 90 degree angle to the edge, **5**. You'll need approximately 7 feet of sidewalks to line one side of the streets.

Then, cut asphalt streets from black illustration board (with the black core), and attach them to the surface of the hatch with carpenter's glue, **6**. They should be at least 5" wide to accommodate two-way traffic. The roads must align perfectly with the edges of the hatch. Weigh them down with books, so they lie flat as the glue dries. Then draw a center line with a white dressmaker's pencil. Trim the sidewalk strips to length to fit alongside the roads, but don't glue them

14

While the paint is still wet, sprinkle on fine green or yellow turf. Then add clumps of coarse turf to make flowers, bushes, and weeds. You can also add a few colorful trees in the yard.

15

To complete the landscaped house lot, use carpenter's glue to secure the walkways and driveways at their specified locations.

16

Additional details, including figures, vehicles, and smaller structures, help bring a scene to life. Use high-tack adhesive to secure these items on the removable hatch.

in place yet. Finally, cut large pieces of white illustration board to fill the remaining area of the hatch, but don't glue them down yet either.

Decide where you want the houses to be placed, **7**. I chose three recently-produced plastic Lionelville houses.

These nicely detailed structures have interior lights and are finished in realistic colors. Their only major fault is the absence of foundations, but we will remedy this deficiency shortly.

Outline the locations of the houses on the white illustration board with a soft

lead pencil. Be sure they line up square to the street. Then draw lines where you wish to place driveways and front walks, **8**. Remove the illustration board from the hatch and cut out these areas.

Now cut strips of black illustration board to make asphalt driveways and

17 This photo shows one completed hatch installed over the layout opening. When the adjacent hatch is scenicked and installed, it will cover the exposed section of pink foam board at left.

18 Here, both hatches are installed. Pay careful attention when aligning the edges, and no one will detect the neighborhood's secret—that two access hatches lie beneath.

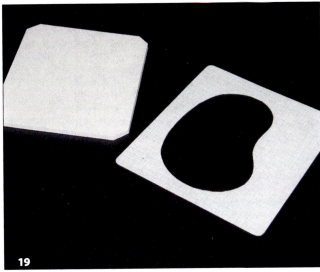

19

For layouts set in summer, an in-ground pool is a fun addition to a yard. Begin by simply cutting a kidney-shaped outline into a thin sheet of styrene.

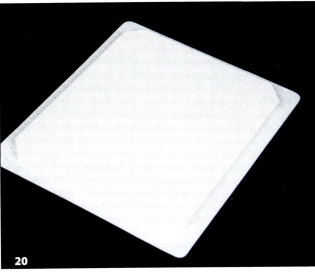

20

Use carpenter's glue to secure the thin plastic pool outline to a scrap piece of foam core board. Clip the corners of the board for easier installation.

21

After allowing the pieces to dry, use a hobby knife with a No. 11 blade to trim the center of the foam core board to match the shape of the pool.

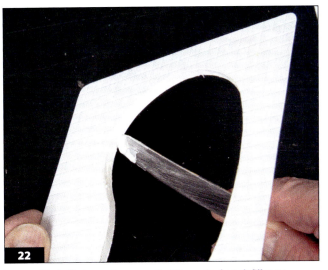

22

Use a table knife to apply a smooth, thin coat of crack filler or drywall compound along the rough-cut edges of the foam core board. Lightly sand the edges when they are dry.

gray strips for concrete walks that fit in the cutout slots, **9**. Be sure to draw in expansion joints on the sidewalks with a pencil. When fitting the driveways and sidewalks, as shown in photo **9**, the front walk stops at the edge of the white illustration board. The driveways are longer because driveways normally interrupt sidewalks and extend all the way to the street.

Set aside the driveways and front walks for now. Use carpenter's glue to attach the pieces of white illustration board to the hatch, butted tightly against the sidewalks next to the roads. Be sure not to glue the sidewalks down, however. Weight the boards with books, and when they are dry, remove the sidewalks and set them aside until after the lawns are added.

Flowers and lawns

The next step is optional, but it adds to the realism and aesthetics of the scene. Construct a foundation for each house with thin strips of balsa or basswood to fit just inside the outlines you drew previously, **10**. Cut the strips with a razor saw (a miniature miter box helps keep the edges square) and glue them to the illustration board. Paint the strips gray to simulate concrete.

Now decide how you plan to landscape the properties, and pencil in such things as flower beds and pathways. Fill in these areas with brown paint. While the paint is still wet, sprinkle it with brown turf, **11**. Select shades of paint and turf that look like either rich soil or pine chips, your choice. Use a small block of wood to press the turf firmly into the paint, **12**. When the paint is dry, vacuum up the excess turf.

The lawns come next. Paint the areas surrounding the houses with a gray-brown paint, not the deep brown you used for the flower beds, **13**. Sprinkle green turf over the wet paint,

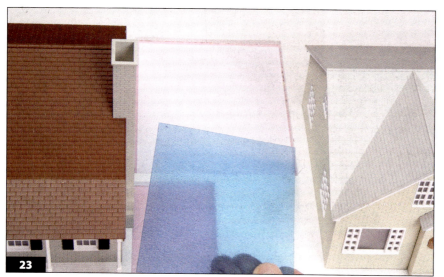

Cut out a rectangular section in the landscaping, fill that section with a piece of white paper, and follow with a thin piece of light blue plastic.

Place the kidney-shaped pool section into the rectangular opening. It isn't necessary to glue the pool in place.

Add swimmers and sunbathers, a raft, and a beach umbrella to help bring the backyard pool party to life.

press it down with a wooden block, and let it dry. Work in small areas at a time—latex paint dries very quickly on the paper surface of the illustration board, and it must stay wet long enough for the turf to adhere. Now you can see why we have delayed gluing in the driveways and sidewalks—to avoid getting paint on them while putting in the lawns.

If you look around your own neighborhood, you will no doubt notice that not all homeowners take good care of their lawns. Some fertilize regularly, water during dry spells, and do battle with dandelions and other weeds. Others simply let Mother Nature have her way. I chose several different shades of turf to duplicate the differences between the well-kept and neglected lawns that you are likely to encounter on a residential street.

Imitation turf comes in many different textures, from very fine for well-manicured grass to thick and coarse for woods and small bushes. Use coarse clumps to make flowering bushes, **14**, and hold them in place with matte medium. You can add flowers by dabbing the tops of the clumps with colored paint, such as the red and white blossoms shown in the photo. You can also purchase ready-made flowering shrubs from hobby suppliers.

Don't forget to add a few trees. The highly detailed red maple seen in photo **14** came from a firm that makes architectural models, but there are many less expensive options. A recent Scenic Express catalog, for example, devotes 28 pages to prefabricated trees and do-it-yourself kits that represent every species, season, and climate to be found in North America. A layout can never have too many trees, and you can buy them in bulk at reasonable prices.

Finishing touches

Now it's time to reinstall the sidewalks, front walks, and driveways. **15**. Wherever a driveway extends all the way to the road, cut the sidewalks to fit on either side. Glue them in place and put the houses on their foundations. The houses must be glued down

26

To help create the illusion of distance at the back of my layout, I placed a variety of ceramic and wooden structures that are somewhat undersized for O gauge.

27

Similar to the construction of the hidden access hatch, you can use foam core illustration board to assemble an entire block of a neighborhood.

to keep them attached when you lift out the hatch. Use household cement or glue intended for plastic models—a small dab on each corner is sufficient to hold them. If you want the houses to be lighted, don't forget to run the wires through holes in the foam core board and the rigid foam insulation hatch.

Small details give life to a scene, **16**. Grandpa sits in his rocker reading the newspaper as the mailman fends off an aggressive German shepherd. Another pet emerges from his doghouse next to the garage to see what the commotion is all about, while the homeowner proudly washes his shiny new 1951 Studebaker. These items must be

firmly attached to the hatch. Woodland Scenics (www.woodlandscenics.com) makes a product called Accent Glue that works well for this purpose. It can be removed from most surfaces without leaving a mark if you want to change the layout at a later date.

Photo **17** shows the completed hatch in place on the layout. The exposed pink foam insulation board at left will be covered when the adjoining hatch is lowered into place.

You can check the alignment of the hatches by looking at them from above, **18**. If you take care to ensure that all of the edges line up exactly with the permanent portions of the layout, no one will notice the hatches at all.

Swimming pools

Features that add life to a residential area are easy to add at any time when your houses are mounted on foam core illustration board. One popular extra is a swimming pool. To add one, you will need a piece of thin plastic hobby flooring material with an embossed tile pattern and a slightly smaller rectangle of illustration board. Cut out a kidney-shaped pool outline, or any other shape you like, in the plastic, **19**. Trim the corners of the illustration board as shown in photo **19**, which will make it easier to install on the layout.

Glue the illustration board to the underside of the plastic sheet with

28

After painting and covering the foam core board with fine turf, reinstall the streets, front walks, and driveways. In this neighborhood, I did not add sidewalks along the street.

29

Return the buildings to their foundations and then add fences, trees, shrubs, hedges, vehicles, and other details to complete the busy neighborhood.

carpenter's glue or, if you are in a hurry, contact cement. Center it carefully, **20**. When it is dry, turn it over and carefully cut out the center of the illustration board to match the shape of the pool, **21**.

The foam core of the board will be slightly rough where you cut it. Apply a thin coat of crack filler or drywall compound with a table knife to smooth it out, **22**. Sand it lightly when it is dry. You can paint it if you wish, but the white filler material looks fine just as it is.

On the illustration board on which your house is mounted, decide where you want the pool to be located and cut out a rectangle just slightly

smaller than the plastic surface of the pool area, **23**. You can do this either before or after the grass is added. Place a rectangle of white paper in the hole. Now cut a sheet of plastic water to fit this area. Scenic Express offers several different versions of this thin material. Choose a light blue color so it resembles chlorinated pool water.

Drop the kidney-shaped pool assembly into the hole on top of the plastic water, **24**. You don't have to glue it in place. In fact, if you haven't added the lawn yet, you will need to be able to remove it. Add swimmers, sunbathers, a raft, and a beach umbrella, and the job is done, **25**.

Creating the illusion of distance

There's another trick you can use for creating neighborhoods at the back of a layout. Almost any modeler would like to have a bigger layout, but often it can't be done because of space constraints. To give your layout a larger appearance, you can use a technique called forced perspective. It consists of placing undersized structures at the back of a layout to fool the eye into thinking they are farther away.

For the back of my layout, I selected an eclectic assortment of ceramic and wooden buildings that are somewhat undersized for O gauge, **26**. With the techniques described in this and other chapters, you can use

In this completed scene, Grandma takes advantage of the nice weather to do her knitting while her daughter sweeps the front walk clean.

Lift-out bridge using GarGraves or Ross track

This truss bridge is long enough to span a door opening, yet light enough to be lifted out of the way.

Rather than using elaborate wiring, I used brass rod extensions to route electrical current over the track on the lift-out bridge.

When the bridge is in place, the rails rest on top of the brass rods. The track should fit tightly over the rails.

You may have to provide access to your layout if it blocks the doorway of the room. Some designs use lift-out, tilt-up, or swinging-gate sections to reach areas of a layout that otherwise would be inaccessible.

To span the distance between door openings and provide access into the room, install a bridge that can be lifted and removed easily,

such as a double-wide truss bridge (948K) manufactured by the Hundred Year Bridge Co. The bridge spans 47½" and is built from 20-gauge steel to support O or S gauge trains. More importantly, even with track, the bridge is still light enough to lift.

It is easy to connect power to the bridge if you are using track with hollow rails, such as Ross or GarGraves. Insert

sections about 1" long of ³⁄₆₄"-diameter brass rod into the flange area underneath each rail at the approach to the bridge and solder the rods in place.

Next, use a flathead screw-driver to widen the underside flange of each rail extending from the bridge. When the bridge is in place, these rails rest on top of the brass rods. To assure the best electrical

contact possible, the track should fit snugly over the rods.

Slide the bridge and attached tracks forward until the rails fit tightly against the ends of the permanent layout tracks. After repeating the same procedure at the other end of the bridge, you will end up with an attractive and easily removable means of crossing a doorway.

31

I especially enjoy creating vignettes that capture everyday life. Here, I have modeled a homeowner interacting with the trash collector as he tends to his work.

them to create a whole neighborhood in record time, as far from the front of the layout as possible. Lay out the streets, cut out pieces of illustration board to adjoin them, arrange the houses, and cut out slots for driveways and front walks. Glue the illustration board in place.

Remove the houses and streets and complete the landscaping, **27**. You'll be surprised at how quickly this can be done—I finished all of the lawns in this area of the layout in less than an hour. Use several shades of paint and different colors of turf for variety.

Replace the streets, along with strips of gray and black illustration board to make the front walks and driveways, and add the houses, **28**. To save time, I didn't bother with sidewalks—not all neighborhoods have them, and they would be hard to see at such a distance from the front.

Now add fences, trees, shrubs and hedges, and other details normally found along the side of the road, **29**. I included speed limit and other signs, garbage cans, and fire plugs. Include vehicles and people doing ordinary everyday things. The red signs are scale-sized Burma Shave signs from the 1950s. These bits of clutter need not be highly detailed, since they will be viewed from a distance, but they add to an overall impression of a busy neighborhood.

It's fun to create little scenes of everyday life, such as the shoppers waiting for the taxi in photo **29**. Grandma is taking advantage of the nice weather to do her knitting out-doors, **30**, while her daughter is busy sweeping the walk. Down the street, a homeowner watches as the local sanitation department stops by to empty his garbage can, **31**. And at the other

end of town, school is out and the bus is just arriving to take the children home, **32**.

To increase the effectiveness of forced perspective, avoid running large diesels or articulated steamers in close proximity to these small buildings. Choose diminutive motive power and rolling stock instead, such as an MTH Climax locomotive hauling a string of skeleton log cars, **33**. Compare the size of the houses in the background with the larger roofs of the houses in the foreground. Notice how the upper level houses appear to be much farther away, when in reality the distance between them is only a few feet.

So far, all of the scenery has been installed on top of the layout table. But in real life, some things extend under ground. We'll look at creating some scenic effects below the surface of the table in the next chapter.

32

Small scenes of everyday events add interest to a layout. In this scene at the far end of town, the school bus arrives just in time to ferry students home from the small schoolhouse.

33

To improve the effectiveness of forced perspective, avoid using large locomotives in close proximity to small buildings. Here, a Climax locomotive pulls a load of logs over a large trestle and looks in proportion to the houses behind it.

CHAPTER FIVE

1

Ponds, water, and below-grade scenery

Using foam insulation board as a train layout tabletop makes it possible to create variations in terrain level by simply adding layers of foam or carving away chunks. I made this pond scene by carving into the foam using a hot wire tool.

One of the most significant advantages of a rigid foam layout top is the ease with which you can dig out areas to include scenic features below grade, such as lakes, rivers, ponds, and gullies. To show you how easily this can be done, let's create an ol' swimmin' hole, nestled into an unused corner of the layout, **1**.

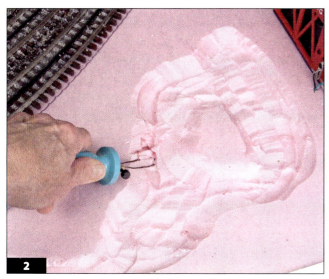

A round-tipped blade fitted to a hot wire tool makes it easy to carve out a shallow pond.

After carving out the pond profile, coat the area with a layer of drywall compound.

Allow the compound to dry before painting. While the paint is wet, add brown turf, sand, and stones along the shoreline.

Scenery manufacturer Scenic Express offers supplies for adding cattails, reedy stalks, and miscellaneous debris to a pond.

The ol' swimmin' hole

A lake, pond, or swimming hole is easy to build. With a round-tipped blade mounted in a hot wire tool, carve out a shallow pond, **2**. Note that I've left a small raised area in the middle, which will become an island. You need not dig down too deeply. You can create the illusion of depth of water by the way you paint the bed of the pond.

Coat the area with a layer of drywall compound, **3**. This layer should be extra thick because it has to contain the water without allowing it to leak through into the foam. The surface can be smooth or rough—it doesn't matter because the bottom of the pond will be covered with gravel and miscellaneous debris.

When the drywall compound has cured, and after filling any cracks that develop, use various colors of paint to cover the bottom. I used light blue for the swimming area where the bed of the pond might be sandy and the water would be relatively clean, and muddy brown for the perimeter and swampy area. While the paint is still wet, sprinkle some gray-brown turf and light-colored sand and rocks along the shoreline, **4**.

For the swampy area of the ol' swimmin' hole, I used some of the supplies that came with a Reeds and Cattails Kit from Scenic Express (EX0247). In addition to some exquisitely formed cattails, this kit contains lichen, reedy stalks, and other materials

that you can use to simulate a backwater area, **5**. Following the instructions that come with the kit can help you create a convincing scene.

Plant the reeds, cattails, and debris in a generous layer of matte medium, **6**. (Matte medium looks white when applied, but turns clear when dry.) Grass and weeds have grown up along the banks, and rocks and submerged branches surround the island. All of these turf products are easy to add—just sprinkle them over wet dirt- or sand-colored paint and allow everything to dry. I also added a dirt path between the pond and the train tracks and covered the low-lying island in the middle of the pond with weedy vegetation.

6 In this photo, reeds and cattails are secured into place using a generous layer of matte medium.

7 After allowing the paint and matte medium to dry overnight, pour two-part resin in the pond to model water.

8 You can use foam core illustration board to model a house foundation. Construct a basement floor, walls, and an inside stairway.

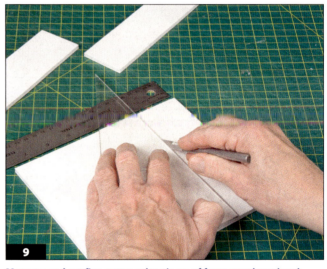

9 Measure and cut five rectangular pieces of foam core board and assemble them into the foundation.

Once the paint is dry, the scene is ready for you to pour the water, which is a two-part chemical compound that comes with the Reeds and Cattails Kit, **7**. It is important to mix the two parts thoroughly to ensure that everything will dry thoroughly and set hard. If you need more water, several similar products are available from various manufacturers that make very convincing water.

The compound is quite viscous and flows slowly, but it will seek its own level and work its way in among the reeds and cattails to cover the rocks and debris. Be sure everything on the bottom is firmly attached before pouring. Use extra matte medium to hold down anything that seems to be loose,

or it will float to the surface when you pour in the water.

The Reeds and Cattails Kit comes with a small straw that is used to eliminate bubbles from the surface. Blow gently through the straw all across the surface of the water until it appears uniformly smooth. As it dries, the water will darken in the debris-filled areas of the pond.

To make the swimmin' hole come to life, you will need to add a variety of details to the scene such as several trees, including one on the little island, people of all ages enjoying the water, a pair of fearless raccoons, and a dog, **1**. I made the No Swimming sign using a word processing program on

my computer and printed it out in an 8-point font.

Moving in

Here's another fun idea for a scene that involves below-grade scenery. A few years ago, Corgi (www.corgi.co.uk) released an interesting house-moving set, consisting of a small home resting on a trailer and pulled by a truck (T989). Why not create an empty lot on your layout with a basement foundation, where the house movers can deliver their burden?

Cut a piece of illustration board to fill an unused corner of the layout where the house will be located, just as you did for the homes in Chapter 4.

To assemble the foam core into a basement, you can use contact cement as well as model glue, rubber cement, or carpenter's glue.

Attach thin strips of balsa or basswood to the perimeter of the rectangle to simulate sills at the top of the foundation.

Let the glue along the sill pieces dry thoroughly, add a stairway, and then coat the entire foundation with gray, concrete-colored paint.

To install the foundation, first outline its shape on the tabletop. Then carve along the outline to create an opening for the foundation.

Also make a length of sidewalk from a strip of gray illustration board. Remove a rectangle the same size as the perimeter of the house to make room for the foundation, **8**. The next step is to construct a basement floor, four basement walls, and an inside stairway.

Foam illustration board is an excellent material for making simple structures, **9**. Measure and cut out five rectangular pieces for the walls and floor of the building's foundation and glue them together with carpenter's glue, contact cement, plastic model glue, or rubber cement from a stationery store, **10**. All of these products work well to fasten pieces of this material together, although the carpenter's glue takes the longest to dry, so avoid it if you are in a hurry. The side walls should be about 2" high, representing a typical 8-foot foundation.

Now glue the foundation into the rectangular opening of the vacant lot panel. The walls should protrude a scale foot (¼") or more above the top surface. Glue thin strips of basswood or balsa around the perimeter of the foundation to simulate sills, **11**.

Build a staircase out of ¾"-wide strips of illustration board. Each descending strip should be a scale 9" (³⁄₁₆") longer than the one above it. It will take 10 strips to complete the stairway. Install it in one corner of the foundation, **12**. Paint everything gray to simulate concrete.

To place the foundation on the layout, you will have to cut a hole in the tabletop for it to fit into, **13**. Be sure to put the hole in the right place. Remember the old adage—measure twice and cut once. Complete the scene with your choice of turf, grass, or piles of dirt. Add a few workmen and a wheelbarrow, and drive the truck and trailer up to the lot.

Now that your miniature people have places to live and play, they need roads to travel on. Foam core illustration board is the perfect material for this. Let's build some city streets and blend them in with accessories that have raised bases. We'll also examine how to construct grade crossings.

CHAPTER SIX

1

Adding city scenery

It takes more than a few large structures to turn a town into a bustling big-city scene. As evident in this photo, in-street tracks, sidewalks, figures, vehicles, signs, and other authentic details bring this urban setting to life.

Given the limited time and money we have to build a layout, it's easy to gloss over some essential details, especially in city scenes. But after a while, unrealistic visual cues—empty storefronts, a street without sidewalks, or oversized building foundations and lampposts—may start to bother you. Fortunately, these problems can be corrected easily and inexpensively with simple and effective urban scenery, **1**.

Study the differences in these before (top) and after (bottom) photos. Making numerous small changes, including the addition of streets, sidewalks, and window dressing, brought this city scene to life. These photos show Ross switches and GarGraves track.

Use black foam core illustration board to represent freshly poured asphalt streets. The 3/16"-thick sheets work best for this application.

Cut the black foam core board into streets with a hobby knife and a metal straight edge.

Cut strips of scrap foam core board to use as shims to raise the streets to the level of accessory bases.

If you look at photo **3**, and compare it to photo **2**, you can see how, with just a few supplies and some basic modeling techniques, I turned an assortment of buildings into a colorful and convincing scene. Instead of empty storefronts, there are rooms behind the glass. The paved streets, lined by sidewalks, and the trolley line are separated from the freight tracks by a retaining wall. The trolley line's rails are flush with the top of the street's blacktop. And everything seems to be in believable proportions. These and other final details, however minor, are important to your layout. Following these easy tips, you can add the smaller details that bring life to your layout.

Streets and sidewalks

For city scenes, you can simulate freshly poured asphalt streets quickly and easily with black foam core illustration board, **4**. The 3/16"-thick sheets are rigid yet lightweight, have a smooth surface, and come in various sizes. (I used 20" x 30" sheets.) While the color is somewhat unnaturally dark, because asphalt weathers to a

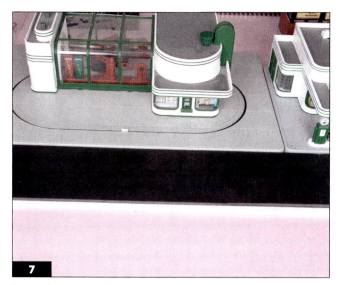

7 Fasten the streets to the shims with carpenter's glue and weight them until they dry.

8 Draw roadway markings with a white fabric pencil or use yellow and white paints or pinstripe tape.

9

10

Many toy train accessories, including this American Flyer lamppost, have oversize features. To hide the large base of a vintage lamppost, install foam core sidewalks along the roadway.

lighter gray as it ages, I like the strong contrast the black color produces. This product comes in two versions, one with a white foam core and one with a black core. The black-core type is best because, if any of the cut edges show, they will blend right in. Light gray works best for concrete sidewalks.

Begin by carefully marking your streets on the foam core boards. Measure carefully before cutting. The minimum width for a street in O gauge is about 6". Add an extra 1¾" to each side of the street for parking, where permitted. Sidewalks vary in width from 4 to 8 feet in the real world, which translates into 1"–2" strips of gray board. Obviously,

keep the width uniform in your city area. Cut the boards using a hobby knife with a No. 11 blade and a metal straightedge to guide your cuts, **5**. The narrow No. 11 blade also allows you to cut irregular shapes, such as rounded curbs for street corners.

Scene leveling

Foam core boards can also be used as scene-leveling shims to raise streets to the height of accessories, grade crossings, and trolley tracks. Scenery shims also help camouflage the oversized foundation bases on many accessory buildings, which have bases of varying thickness. Foam core shims make such adjustments easy. You can shim under

one building while leaving another building alone to balance the difference in their heights.

Building up the streets

If you use operating accessories with bases that are higher than the streets, your model cars can't drive into them. My layout features an MTH gas station, car wash, fire house, and Mel's Diner as well as a Lionel hobby shop and a Ford dealership with high bases. Instead of cutting holes in the foam to sink them down to the level of the tabletop, I built up the streets instead.

Foam core illustration board is ³⁄₁₆" thick, and with an additional ³⁄₁₆" layer underneath, the streets will rise almost

Add details such as fire hydrants, phone booths, vending machines, and figures to the sidewalks to complete a bustling city scene. You can find a wide variety of figures in many action poses.

To submerge trolley tracks into a street, glue ½"-wide black foam core strips between the rails.

Test-fit the installation to ensure that the trolley moves freely. Use a hobby knife to trim any areas that interfere with the wheels.

up to the level of the accessories. In fact, for extra realism, these accessories will appear as if they have a slightly raised curb lining the pavement.

To build up the streets, first cut narrow strips of illustration board to use as shims and then glue them to the table, **6**. I recommend using carpenter's glue (slow-drying) or contact cement

(quick-drying, if you are in a hurry). Next, run a thin bead of glue along the tops of the strips.

Install the streets on top of these strips, **7**. If you use carpenter's glue, weigh the streets down with books or even a locomotive until the glue dries. Butt the accessories tightly against the edges of the streets. Don't forget to

make holes in the tabletop to accommodate the wires that are necessary to make these clever toys work.

Using the same method, you can surround the accessories with vacant lots, lawns, or parking lots made from illustration board. Cover them with grass or dirt where appropriate (as described in Chapters 2 and 3), as

14 You can install foam retaining walls to separate main line tracks from roads. Use a hobby knife to trim these walls to fit.

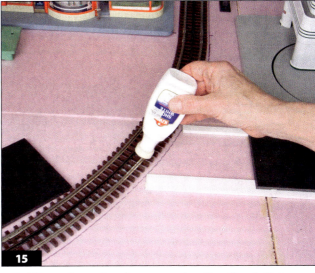

15 To build a grade crossing along a curved section of track, first spread white shoe polish along the rails.

16 Next, press the black foam core roadway section over the top of the rails covered with shoe polish.

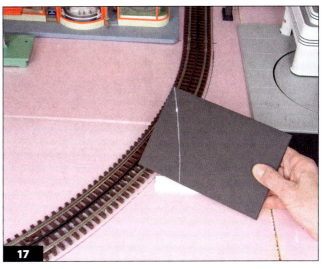

17 Remove the roadway section from the rails to reveal the white lines that define the cut marks for an exact fit.

shown beside the MTH fire station, **4**. Shim everything up to the level of the accessory bases with narrow strips of illustration board underneath, the same as you did with the streets.

Another advantage of using illustration board for this kind of scenery is that you can cut into it to make room for such things as crossing warning lights (lower right in photo **4**). Also note that the raised street is at exactly the right height to form a grade crossing where the track bisects the street.

Detailing streets and sidewalks

On the streets, don't forget to add lines on the pavement to represent directional lanes, crosswalks, and parking spaces. I drew these with a white fabric pencil, but you can use yellow and white paint or tape to model the striping patterns that you want to follow, **8**.

The gray foam core sidewalks require some added attention. Before installing the sidewalks on the shims, draw lines for expansion joints and the curb with a pencil. Fit them loosely in place, and figure out where you want to place detail items, especially lampposts.

On my layout, the lampposts are vintage American Flyer. They're a bit oversized for O gauge, but they provide a nice period atmosphere. Still, I felt compelled to hide the unrealistically large bases.

The foam core sidewalks make it easy to hide these bases. Measure and cut a hole in the sidewalk—in this case an octagonal opening—to fit over the lamppost, **9**. Drill holes in the layout table to accommodate the lampost wires and glue the sidewalks in place, **10**.

Add details such as fire hydrants, phone booths, and newspaper vending machines, plus plenty of people and pets, to your sidewalks, **11**. There's a wide variety of people available for O gauge, so you can add as much character as you want to your street scenes.

Trolley tracks

If you run a trolley or train in your streets as I did, you need to elevate

Use a hobby knife to trim the roadway section along the outer edge of the white cut line.

Trim a ½"-wide strip of paper from the underside of the roadway section to accommodate the height of the track ties.

Install the roadway next to the rails. Use foam core strips to shim the road. Then tuck the edge of the roadway under the railhead.

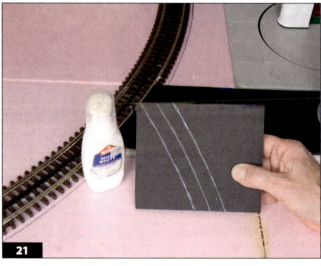

To complete the roadway between the rails, first coat all three rails with shoe polish and press another roadway section over the rail tops.

the streets and respective scenery even with the top of the trolley rails. Most track systems available today, including GarGraves and Ross Custom Switches, measure about ⅜" from the bottom of the ties to the top of the rails. So you need to raise the ³⁄₁₆"-thick streets another ³⁄₁₆" to create a flush surface.

On GarGraves track, the ties also measure ³⁄₁₆" tall, so the ties themselves serve as matching shims. I placed the black foam core street sections, as well as narrow strips between the ties, directly on the track to effectively bury it in asphalt, **12**. I merely added a beveled edge to allow the street boards to clear the rail base. I also left some clearance on

the inside of the running rails for the trolley's wheel flanges.

The ½"-wide foam strips between the rails don't need much glue to hold them in place—a dab every 10 ties or so is sufficient. However, make sure that the end of each strip is secure. Again, apply weight until the glue is dry.

When completed, the buried track shouldn't hamper the trolley's path. You may want to test your trackwork just to make sure the trolley moves freely along the rails, **13**.

If you have tracks running adjacent to the street, you may want to separate them from the street somehow. I chose to add a short stone retaining wall, such as FL4150 or FL4151

offered by Scenic Express, **14**. This foam wall is easy to cut with a hobby knife so you can shape it to fit around difficult obstacles, such as the switch machine on a Ross Custom Switches double crossover. Here, the retaining wall also disguises the difference in height between the street and the top of the train table on which the track is mounted.

Grade crossings

Wherever a street must cross the tracks, simply cut the illustration board to lie against the rails on top of the ties. This is easy if the track is straight, but somewhat more difficult if the track is curved. However, there's an easy way

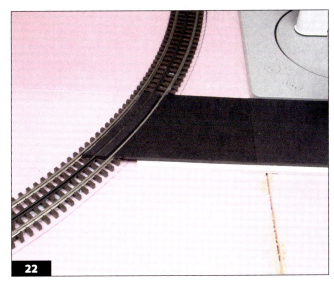

22

Trim the roadway section using a sharp hobby knife. Be sure to trim the cut pieces so they don't interfere with the train wheels.

23

Paint the beveled edge of the illustration board with a thick coat of brown paint and then add coarse green turf to simulate weeds.

24

Use a small block of wood to tamp the turf into the wet paint. After drying, vacuum up any loose pieces of turf.

25

Use a spoon to fill the area between the scenery board and track with gray ballast.

to mark the illustration board in order to cut it for an exact fit. Spread white liquid shoe polish on top of the rail, **15**. Then press the illustration board down against the shoe polish, **16**. This will transfer a white line to the underside of the street, **17**. (Don't forget to wipe the remaining polish off the rails before you run the trains again.)

Then take a hobby knife fitted with a No. 11 blade and carefully cut along the outer edge of the white line, **18**. On the underside of the board, remove a ½"-wide strip of the paper and about half the thickness of the foam core to clear the ties, **19**.

Turn the board over and install it next to the track on top of illustration

board shims to bring it to the proper level, **20**. Tuck the curved edge under the top of the rail.

To enable your drivers to cross the tracks in relative comfort, you will need strips of asphalt between the rails. First, coat all three rails with shoe polish and press another length of street material down against them, **21**. Cut out the black areas between the lines and install them between the rails, **22**. You may need to trim them somewhat to be sure the flanges on the train wheels have enough clearance to pass through without binding.

Other illustration board scenery panels, such as grassy areas, can be cut to fit around the grade crossings.

Where the edges of the scenery stop short of the roadbed, there is an easy way to finish these areas. Wherever your illustration board scenery borders the track, bevel the edge at about a 45-degree angle before you glue the board to the layout so it slopes down toward the track. Lay on a thick coat of paint to receive the scenery material. The vegetation that lines a ballasted roadbed is often somewhat rough and weedy, so choose coarse turf for this area, and perhaps mix it with other debris, such as broken branches and small rocks. Sprinkle the material over the wet paint, **23**, and press it in place with a small block of wood, **24**. Vacuum up anything that doesn't stick.

26

Work the ballast between the ties and then use a small paintbrush to sweep the excess from the tops of the ties.

27

Secure the ballast on both sides of the track by applying matte medium with an eyedropper.

28

Allow the matte medium to dry and then apply more ballast between the rails. You don't have to secure this ballast as it will be held in place by the ballast on the sides.

Fill the area between the scenery board and the track with ballast, **25**. Work it in well between the ties and then sweep away the excess from the tops of the ties with a small paintbrush, **26**.

Secure the ballast on both sides of the track by applying matte medium with an eyedropper, **27**. When the matte medium has dried, sprinkle more ballast between the rails, **28**, but you don't have to glue it down. The ballast along the sides will keep it from moving around or escaping from under the ties.

Setting scenes

On my layout, the main emphasis of the scenery, as in the real world, is upon living space for the miniature occupants. At last count, more than 275 people (and a fair number of pets and other wildlife) populate my layout. But these figures aren't randomly placed around the layout. They're positioned to re-create miniature depictions of everyday activity, **29**. I designed each scene on the layout to tell an interesting story. Buildings aren't very interesting by themselves, and it doesn't take much to turn a business establishment into a human-interest story. A row of used cars in front of an auto agency is hardly worth a second glance until you add a fast-talking salesman, extolling the virtues of an almost-new Thunderbird.

Once roads and sidewalks are in place, you can add structures, people, vehicles, and other details. It's a good idea to shim up all of the streets and surrounding properties in suburban or residential areas, just as you did next to the operating accessories to put them at the proper level.

City scenes need a lot of detail to be convincing. An urban area is naturally more crowded than a town or country scene. Buildings are closer together, and there's a lot more traffic. Fill a scene with interesting details to give an impression of bustling activity and a prosperous citizenry, **30**. For example, on just one busy street corner of this layout, you will find one police officer directing traffic—the MTH traffic lights must be temporarily out of order—while another patrols on

29

See if you can spot the people who bring this scene to life—a locomotive engineer, a woman driving a convertible, a car wash attendant, a man leaving the hobby shop, and a woman mailing a letter.

his motorcycle. A young family is out for a stroll, and a city sewer worker is emerging from a manhole, protected by a portable barrier and a Men at Work sign. All of these details can be held in place with Accent Glue (Woodland Scenics). There are also plenty of cars and a bus on hand to complete the scene.

You will probably want to include a depot, such as the Lioneltown Station (No. 137). You will need commercial establishments and transportation facilities—there's a Lionel hobby shop next to an MTH Greyhound bus station (No. 30-9040), **29**. And don't forget a hotel for travelers (the four-story red brick building further down the street). Other buildings and accessories crowd the area to the right, which gives purpose to the rail traffic passing through the city.

Fighting a fire. The MTH operating House on Fire (No. 30-9139) attracts a lot of attention on a layout, with its flickering red fire inside and smoke pouring out the roof, **31**. It also

contains a miniature water pump that sends a spray of water out the fireman's hose and through the burned-out section of the roof. If you choose to take advantage of this level of realism, however, be sure the water doesn't leak onto the scenery, as it will damage the paper surfaces of the illustration board. Two gallant firefighters with hoses struggle to control the blaze inside this MTH house on fire. One of their colleagues just rescued a teenager from the second story and carries her toward the ladder and then down to safety. A number of bystanders and a pair of firehouse Dalmatians watch the excitement. These figures are from Arttista and MTH. The vintage emergency vehicles made by Ertl (www.ertltoys.com) and Matchbox (www.matchbox.com) add further interest to the scene.

Selling cars. This shrewd car dealer knows how to attract buyers to his Ford dealership, **32**. Each Saturday he invites local college students to wash cars in front of his establishment as a fund-raising effort for their clubs and

organizations. Bikinis are optional, but strongly encouraged, and the dealer has noticed a decided increase in the number of male customers who visit his showroom on weekends. The figures are from Arttista Accessories (www.arttista.com). The Lionel car dealership comes complete with three 1950s-era Ford automobiles for the showroom, but you will need more if you want to include a used car inventory outside. You will also have to add parking facilities to the dealership. Choose gray illustration board to simulate a concrete parking area as shown or use black if you prefer the appearance of asphalt.

Along the seaside. An Atlantic Canadian railroad would seem incomplete without a seaside vista, **33**. In this scene, an old seaman watches a crew repairing the road (left), and the trees bend under the force of a brisk ocean wind. The Lionel Big Bay lighthouse (No. 24119) contains sound effects of waves, sea gulls, and a realistic foghorn. Artist Olivia Frampton of Nova Scotia painted this background directly on

30

Building an authentic city scene requires the use of numerous figures, vehicles, and street-level details. Notice how the sidewalk separates the street from the parking area at left.

31

In real life and on toy train layouts, fire scenes always attract attention. This modeled scene features flickering red lights, smoke, and real spraying water.

32

When the car dealership on my layout hosts a car wash, there's no shortage of bikini-clad helpers, vehicles for sale, and interested male customers.

33

A coastal railroad would seem incomplete without a seaside vista like the scene hand-painted on my layout's wall backdrop.

34

When arranged with a purpose, even a large slab of glacial rock can become a focal point of layout scenery.

the room wall. You don't need to make background scenes elaborate or overly detailed. Note how the soft colors in the painting create a feeling of distance as you look out to sea.

On the rock. Near the lighthouse, a young boy waves to his friends from atop a slab of glacial rock, while a policeman directs a Dinky Toy

Chrysler convertible through the intersection, **34**. The Chevrolet Nomad station wagon and Airstream travel trailer are part of a Lionel No. 24164 summer vacation accessory, and the figures are from Arttista and MTH. The prefinished rock formation is one of a wide variety of lightweight scenery items from Scenic Express.

At the park. A favorite spot for the youngest visitors to the layout is the park, which contains swings, teeter-totters, and a merry-go-round, courtesy of this clever Lionel No. 24138 animated playground accessory, **35**.

At the amusement park. Miniature people need recreation too, **36**. I've provided them with their own Lionel

35

Operating accessories like this animated playground from Lionel are easy items to integrate into existing layout scenes. Figures include people of all ages interacting as well as several pets.

animated amusement park, where children can ride the ponies (No. 14210) and mom and dad can play miniature golf (No. 14214). Everyone can try their luck at some games of chance (Nos. 14230, 34158, and 34159) along the midway or take an exhilarating ride on the Scrambler (No. 24179) or pirate ship (No. 14171). Chapter 7 describes how to set up animated accessories.

In the neighborhood. The most effective scenes are often the simplest, where ordinary people do ordinary things, **37**. A portly gentleman assists his wife as she emerges from the family's 1955 Pontiac Safari wagon (Road Champs), and Farmer MacDonald drives slowly into town in his well-preserved 1914 Chevrolet at a safe and sane 10 mph. He's followed closely by a 1940 Ford Woody wagon, its driver irritated by the old man's slow pace. Both cars are from Ertl.

Ballasting track

By adding ballast to your track, it will look more realistic. My greatest pleasure in the toy train hobby doesn't

come from running trains, although I do enjoy that activity, but from building railroads. As a result, I tear down my O gauge layout every two years and experiment with new track plans and scenic techniques.

On my previous layouts I never cemented the ballast in place because I knew I would eventually be taking up the track to rearrange it. I didn't want to face the task of scraping ballast off the ties, so I spread the ballast along the right-of-way and depended on the rest of the scenery to confine it. This method was only partially successful, with the ballast tending to migrate where it wasn't wanted and the layout appearance not being what I hoped for. So, for my latest layout, I devised a method that uses a minimum amount of glue to hold the ballast in place without adhering to the entire length of each tie. The following steps show just how easy great-looking track can be.

Ballast comes in a variety of colors and in fine, medium, or coarse textures. I used Scenic Express EX3405

No. 12 light gray coarse blend for contrast with the dark brown ties of Atlas O track, **38**. For this technique, all you need are your choice of ballast, Scenic Express matte medium transparent scenery cement (No. EX0010), an eyedropper, and a spoon for easy spreading.

Here are a few tips to get you started. First, ballast is like a picture frame—it shouldn't be more interesting to look at than the scene it completes. I favor light gray. Second, in addition to the tools and materials I've already outlined, you'll need to allow plenty of time. Ballasting is simple so there's a temptation to rush through it. Don't fall into that trap. Do a manageable section as neatly as you can, then take a break. Third, make sure no rocks remain on top of the ties—in addition to looking sloppy, it's a no-no on real railroads.

I didn't use a raised roadbed on my current layout for two reasons. First, my railroad is a short line modeled after the local extension of the Canadian Pacific, now known as the Wind-

36

By combining a variety of animated Lionel accessories, you can make an amazing amusement park setting, especially when the accessories can be set flush with the surrounding surfaces.

sor & Hantsport RR. The track in this area is elevated only very slightly above the surrounding terrain. Second, the ties on Atlas O track are ¼" thick, which is high enough (a scale foot) to allow for a shallow shoulder along the edges.

Shape the ballast to slope gradually away from the ties. Use a spoon to spread the ballast along the outer edges of the track and in between the ends of the ties, **39**. A little ballast will migrate under the rails, but don't spread any there yet. With your fingers, shape the ballast to slope away from the track at an angle of about 30 degrees.

My method of gluing the ballast makes it stick to the layout table and just slightly to the ends of the ties, but it doesn't travel any farther. To prevent the medium from getting on the rails or covering the ties, I fill an eyedropper with matte medium and drip it onto the ballast along the shoulder, but not in between the ties, **40**.

The matte medium saturates the ballast and bonds it together, and it's invisible when dry. The glue flow-

ing between the grains of ballast may disturb some of them, but you'll have time to push them back in place with your finger or spoon. At first it will seem like the glue isn't working, as the ballast will still be loose. But when dry, the grains form a rigid wall along the edge of the track.

Since this type of glue is much easier to remove than white glue, it's a simple task to clean the ends of the ties when you take up the track for a new layout.

Whatever you do, don't rush this step! Wait until the glue has completely dried before proceeding. You can now spread the remainder of the ballast between the rails and the ties without using more matte medium, **41**. The solid shoulders of ballast will confine the loose material and keep it from traveling where you don't want it to go.

Double-track main lines may be filled in with ballast or weeds and grass, depending on your railroad's standard of maintenance. You can fill the space between two parallel tracks with more

loose ballast of the same type or a finer blend to simulate gravel, **42**. I used Scenic Express light gray fine blend #20 (No. EX3005). I also sprinkled some coarse turf material to suggest a few weeds, **43**. You won't need any glue here. The finer gravel can't escape from or mix with the ballast that you glued along the ties.

I like a strong contrast between the ballast and the surrounding scenery. For a more muted look, choose one of the other colors available from Scenic Express. They range from pale limestone to dark coke or coal and include red iron ore and brown quartz. When the time comes to change the layout, sweep up the ballast and save it for your next project.

I like the realistic tie spacing and blackened center rail that are features of Atlas O's track. Ballast is the icing on the cake. I know it's one of those tasks that many modelers would like to avoid, but I encourage everyone to give ballast a try. Results like this really are just as easy as the steps I've outlined.

Some of the most effective layout scenes are often the simplest, such as in this neighborhood, where ordinary folks are seen doing ordinary things.

When ballasting this Atlas O track, I used light gray coarse blend ballast from Scenic Express.

Use a spoon to spread the ballast along the outer edges of the ties and in between the ends of the ties.

Adding vehicles

Nothing dates a layout as accurately as automobiles, and your choice in vehicles goes a long way in establishing the era of a scene. I used die-cast metal cars representing models from the late 1950s. You can find a huge

variety of suitable models in a wide range of quality and prices. Vehicles can range from under $10 to more than $100. For O gauge (a 1:48 ratio of model to reality), the closest size are those made in 1:43 scale. Some bus and truck models, such as those

made by Corgi in Great Britain, are 1:50 scale, which is also very close to O gauge. For background areas of a layout, you can use smaller 1:64 proportion vehicles, as they promote a feeling of greater distance and perspective. (They are the correct size for

Load an eyedropper with matte medium and apply drops along the shoulder.

Spread the remainder of the ballast between the rails, but do not apply any additional matte medium.

Fill space between two parallel tracks with more loose ballast or an even finer blend of gravel. Also add coarse turf to represent weeds.

Other areas along the right-of-way may see heavier undergrowth, which can be represented with extra coarse turf.

foreground use with American Flyer and other S scale trains.)

The most expensive vehicles, such as those from Brooklin Models (www.brooklinmodels.co.uk), are highly detailed and best displayed close to the edge of the layout where they may be examined closely. A large assortment of less expensive but well-made cars are available from AutoArt, Corgi, and Matchbox. Even the most economical miniature automobiles, such as those made by Yat-Ming, Road Champs and Road Signature are convincing representations of the real thing. You can also choose from among a number of other manufacturers of miniature vehicles distributed by such companies as Diecast Direct, Inc. (www.diecastdirect.com).

Finishing buildings

Perhaps the most important fine detail is the addition of store interiors to the buildings, **44**. I printed computer-generated images of business, office, and home interiors sized to fit these Ameri-Towne storefronts. They can also be customized to fit virtually any model railroad building.

Admittedly, you may want to find other ways to dress up your windows if you don't want to use a computer and printer. Optionally, you can scour magazines for photos and illustrations, using a color copier to reduce some scenes for your windows.

When you've touched up your urban scenes, you'll have a hard time accepting anything less ever again. With this minimal investment in effort and materials, you'll still have plenty of time left over for the trains you'll want to run through these convincing scenes.

Fitting in accessories

Some accessories have exposed binding posts for connecting the wires, which look very unrealistic. You can hide them several ways. The easiest way is to plant some shrubbery on top, but that isn't always appropriate, depending upon the location. Try to find something to hide the posts

When completing buildings in a city setting, you can use computer-generated graphics to add signs, interior depth, and other details to stores for a realistic touch.

Like the American Flyer lamppost, some operating accessories, both vintage and modern, have oversized features than are easily disguised. Here, I used three hollow plastic barrels to cover unrealistic, yet essential binding post for electrical wiring.

that goes naturally with the scene. For example, I found some small hollow plastic barrels that fit nicely over the binding posts on this Lionel automatic stop-and-start station from the prewar years, **45** and **46**. A hollow packing crate would look good inverted over the posts on an industrial accessory, such as a coal or log loader. Or make little round caps out of aluminum foil and turn the posts into garbage cans. (Imagination is a wonderful thing—give yours plenty of exercise.)

With accessories with round bases or irregular shapes, you can fit the scenery around them by taking advantage of the properties of a foam tabletop, as you'll see in the next chapter.

CHAPTER SEVEN

1

Using animation

Animated accessories add extra interest and fun to any layout, and in recent years Lionel has produced a wide variety of them that show people engaged in recreational activities. They are well detailed, operate smoothly, and add greatly to the realism of any miniature scene, such as the park on my layout, **1**.

When integrated with other layout scenery, an animated accessory can provide just as much excitement, if not more, than an operating toy train. In this scene, viewers will only see a glimpse of a train in the background, but that doesn't diminish the eye-catching action of the amusement park in the foreground.

2

To integrate an amusement park with the scenery, first assemble the accessories in a logical position on the foam tabletop. Then take a digital photo that you can reference later in the construction process.

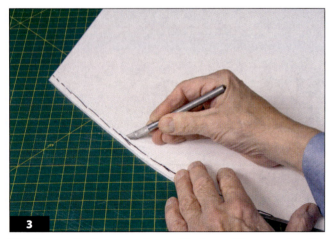

3

Hide the oversized accessory bases with a layer of foam core board. Cut the edges of the foam core at a 45 degree angle.

4

Use medium grit sandpaper to create a smooth edge that is better suited for a transition from scenery to ballast.

Creating an amusement park

An animated amusement park is an especially attractive focal point for a model railroad. There's plenty of noise and activity to entertain your guests. Be sure to locate it near the edge of your viewing area, because some of the action is relatively small—for example, you have to watch very closely to see the golfers swing their clubs as they putt out on the mini-golf course. You won't have any trouble noticing the he-man swing his mallet on the Test of Strength accessory, however, as the bell rings out loud and clear when he scores.

Be sure to wire each accessory with a separate on/off switch. The swing ride, band shell, and carousel all have different music to accompany the action, and this creates cacophony when they all operate at once. The pirate ship ride is also quite noisy, and easily drowns out the little bells that ring when the marksmen succeed in hitting a duck in the shooting gallery.

5

Place the foam core board in the park area, use the reference photo to reposition the accessories, and outline each of them.

6

Remove the accessories and cut openings about ¼" inside the marked outlines. Angle the hobby knife to make beveled cuts.

7

Test the fit of the accessories in each opening as you go. Openings should be snug, but not tight enough to force the board upward.

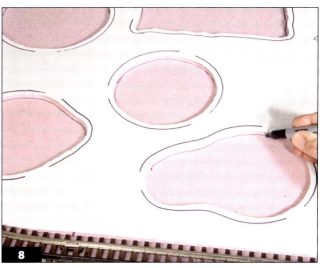

8

Return the foam core to the park area and mark the outline of each opening onto the foam tabletop.

If, for example, you want to create a realistic amusement park with Lionel animations, you can hide the mechanisms that are enclosed in raised plastic bases and blend them together into a unified area.

With a rigid foam insulation tabletop, it's easy to sink the accessories into the board so that they are level with the surrounding scenery. If you have a plywood tabletop, simply cover it with a 1"-thick insulation panel.

These accessories may be worth something someday, and you don't want to get paint or anything else on them that might lessen their value. You have nothing to worry about. The method I'm about to show you will not risk getting scenery paint or any kind of permanent glue or other material on them. The techniques involved are relatively simple. Begin by placing the accessories in a logical pattern of activity, **2**. When you are satisfied with the arrangement, take a photo for reference as you place the accessories.

Hiding bases

It won't surprise you to hear that the key to burying the accessories within the layout is to surround them with foam core illustration board. Using a hobby knife with a No. 11 blade, cut a board to make a scenic panel that will fit the area of your layout where the park will be located. If one board is not large enough, splice two pieces together using glue on their edges and tape on the underside. (Unlike the streets and other areas in the city, the board will not have to be shimmed up.)

If the board is to lie beside a curved track, draw the shape of the curvature with a felt tip marker and cut it out. Bevel the edge at about a 45 degree angle, **3**. Round the upper edge of the beveled cut with medium grit sandpaper, **4**. This will simulate the sloping side of a ditch beside the tracks.

Place this scenic panel on the layout and arrange the accessories on top of it, using your photo for reference. Outline all of the items with a felt tip marker, **5**. Note that some of these items, such as

9

10

Use a hot wire tool to hollow out a shallow space beneath each accessory. Accessories should rise only ³⁄₁₆" above the tabletop.

Place the accessories into the appropriate openings and then add the foam core board. Label the locations that will receive scenery.

11

12

Before adding scenery to the top of the foam core board, first coat the underside with a thin layer of paint.

The paint will cause the board to warp in one direction. Painting the top side will now cause the board to warp in the opposite direction.

the midway shooting gallery (at upper right), will sit on top of the board, while others will be submerged under it.

Cut holes in the board approximately ¼" inside the outlines of only those accessories that have raised bases that you want to hide, **6**. Bevel the edges of the holes at a 45 degree angle so that the bottom of each hole is wider than the opening on top. This will allow the panel to ride up over the curved shoulders of the accessories.

Test fit each accessory in its assigned hole, **7**. The openings in the boards should fit fairly snug but not so tight as to be forced to rise above the surface of the accessory base. If necessary, trim away a little of the foam board on the underside.

When you are satisfied with the fit, place the board on the layout again, but with the accessories removed. Outline all of the holes on the foam board table top with a marker, **8**. Remove the scenery panel again. Using a hot wire foam cutter, hollow out the areas beneath the accessories so that when they are placed on the layout, they will rise only ³⁄₁₆" above the surface, **9**. This will take some trial and error, but don't worry if you cut too deeply. It will be easy to shim up the accessory with cardboard or bits of foam later on if necessary.

Put the accessories into the hollowed out areas and place the scenery board on top of them, **10**. If they all rise just ³⁄₁₆" above the top of the table,

they will now be level with the top of the ³⁄₁₆"-thick illustration board panel. If some are too high, cut a little deeper into the foam tabletop. If some are too low, shim them up. It is essential that the scenery board lie flat on the table at this stage of construction. Add the buildings or accessories that sit on top of the scenery board and make a rough drawing of any scenic elements that you wish to add. Label the areas where grass and dirt paths will be.

The next step is very important. Put a single coat of paint on the underside of the scenery panel, **11**. The paper surface of the foam board will shrink slightly when the paint dries, causing it to warp and become curved, **12**. When

13 Use a variety of fine and coarse turf materials to cover the park grounds. Try to blend the colors to match the accessory bases.

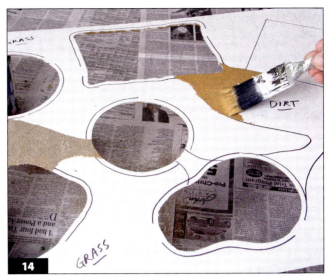

14 Apply a thick coat of brown latex paint to cover the areas where the dirt pathway will go.

15 While the paint is still damp, apply gravel to the painted pathway. Work in short sections and shake the board to better distribute the material.

16 Press the gravel further into the wet painted surface. Again, tilt the board to shake off any excess scenery material.

17 Place wax paper on top of the scenery panel and weigh it down to help it dry flat.

18 To blend the accessories with the scenery, apply rubber cement to the gap between the base of the accessory and the foam core panel.

19 Sprinkle turf and dirt material to match the area surrounding the accessory. Press the material into the tacky rubber cement before it dries.

20 Covering the edge of the base with the same materials provides a well-blended transition between the accessory and the scenery. You can apply additional cement and materials to fill in any bare spots.

21 Place the animated accessories without hidden bases, such as the Duck Shoot, on top of the board. When all of the scenery, small trees, figures, vehicles, and other details are in place, it becomes difficult to tell where the oversized bases on the accessories are.

you apply paint to the upper side of the board later on, the paper surface on that side will also shrink, and the board will warp in the opposite direction, which returns it to being flat. If you do not paint both sides of the board, the resultant warping will make it very dif-ficult to glue the scenery board in place on the layout.

Adding scenery

Once the scenery board is in place, you can add the scenic elements, **13.** You can choose from dozens of shades of grass to duplicate any season of the year, simulated dirt ranging from dark mud to light sand, clumped turf for weedy or overgrown areas, and a number of specialty products for creating fields, deadfall forest areas, and pastures. For my amusement park, I chose

When adding figures, be sure to group them around the animated activities to add more interest. Use tacky glue, such as Woodland Scenics Accent Glue, to hold the figures and other details in place.

a medium green grass, a sandy color for pathways, and a weed mixture for the areas closest to the rail line.

Proceed by covering the pathways that wind through the park. Following the lines you drew when the accessories were in place, lay down a thick base coat of latex paint where the gravel will go, **14**. A medium brown shade that resembles dirt works best in case it shows through anywhere when you are finished.

Sprinkle fine gravel material into the wet paint, **15**. Latex paint dries quickly on the paper surface of the foam board, so don't try to paint too large an area at any one time. Work in small sections. Shake the scenery panel to distribute the scenic material throughout the paint.

Use a small block of wood to press the gravel into the wet paint, **16**. Then tilt the scenery panel and shake it to remove any material that has not stuck

fast. Sweep up the residue and save it for future use. Continue until all of the pathways have been painted and covered. Then repeat the procedure for the grassy areas and the weedy places beside the tracks. (See Chapter 6 for detailed instructions on applying rough vegetation along the sides of the roadbed.)

Blending the accessories
Place wax paper on top of the scenery panel and weigh it down to help it to dry flat, **17**. For weights I used a half-filled container of drywall compound and a plastic bottle filled with paint, both of which have flat bottoms. Avoid using paint cans as weights, because the raised rims on the bottoms will leave circular impressions in the grass and dirt. Books also work well, but don't use too many, as they will cut off air flow and slow the drying process. Use just enough to make the panel flatten out properly.

While the illustration board panel is drying, make holes in the table for the wires and then put the accessories in place. Connect all the wires and test each accessory, as it will be difficult to correct any problems after the scenery panel is installed.

Spread carpenter's glue or contact cement on the underside of the illustration board panel. Be careful not to get the glue too close to the cutouts for the accessories. Lower the panel over the accessories and weight it so it will adhere to the tabletop. Allow plenty of time for the glue to dry completely before removing the weights. (Carpenter's glue takes an especially long time to cure when used to connect illustration board to a rigid foam insulation tabletop. Be patient.)

Now we must blend the accessories in with the scenic panel without doing anything to lessen their value.

23

In some situations, it's possible to bury oversized accessory bases into the foam tabletop and blend the edge with drywall compound and scenery.

24

After blending the accessory base into the tabletop, spread a thin layer of drywall compound over the entire area.

25

Add a thick coat of paint to the drywall compound and then apply a covering of turf and gravel to complete the scene.

We do this with rubber cement, a type of adhesive that works well to hold artificial grass and dirt but which also rubs off completely whenever you decide to remove it. It will not leave any marks on the surfaces of the accessories. With the brush that comes in the bottle, apply rubber cement to the gap between the base of the accessory and the illustration board panel, **18**.

Sprinkle grass and dirt material to match the surrounding area over the cement before it can dry and press it down firmly with your finger, **19**. The accessory will now look as if it is part of the adjoining landscape, **20**. Don't worry if some spots look a little thin, such as where the dirt path meets the upper right side of the pony ride. You can dab on additional rubber cement and scenery material as many times as necessary until everything is properly covered.

Continue to blend in the rest of the accessories and install those that sit on top of the illustration board panel, such as the Duck Shoot, **21**. Add a few trees and, most importantly of all, some people to enjoy the park, **22**. Don't forget to add some human interest details, such as the children buying ice cream from a Good Humor truck. Use Accent Glue to hold everything in place—otherwise the vibration from passing trains will tend to knock the figures over and move small details around.

Adding permanent accessories

If you expect your accessories to become a permanent addition to your layout, you may not be concerned with keeping them in absolutely like-new condition. If that is the case, you can blend them into the layout with drywall compound. When the time comes that you want to remove the accessory and use it elsewhere or put it away, the dried compound can be removed from the plastic accessory with some water and a sharp tool to clean out crevices, although it takes a lot of patience.

This technique is useful in areas where you don't surround the accessory with a layer of foam core illustration board. Photo **23** shows a Lionel

Animated action on a train layout adds interest for viewers. The action can come from something as simple as a vehicle backing out of a parking space.

The secret behind this simple animation is the Tortoise slow-motion switch machine.

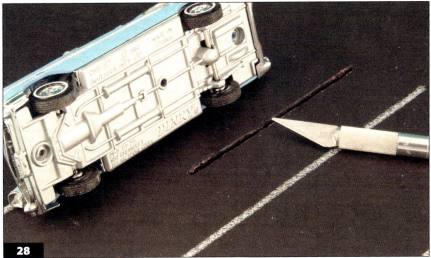

A length of piano wire extends from the switch machine through a slot in the tabletop to fit into a hole in the bottom of the vehicle.

hobo campfire in an area on the layout where gravel, grass, and dirt are applied directly to the foam tabletop. Hollow out a space deep enough to receive the accessory, so it is level at the top. Try to make the hole as close to the circumference of the acces-

sory as possible. Using an ordinary table knife, fill in the area between the insulation board and the sloped shoulder of the accessory with drywall compound.

I placed the Lionel Hobo Campfire near the tracks in an industrial area of

the layout, where the ground would be expected to be somewhat uneven. To simulate these conditions, I coated the entire area with a thin layer of drywall compound, **24**. Then I added paint and scenic material to complete the scene, **25**.

29

The metal rod supplied with the switch machine is too short to use here. Instead, use piano wire to form a longer rod.

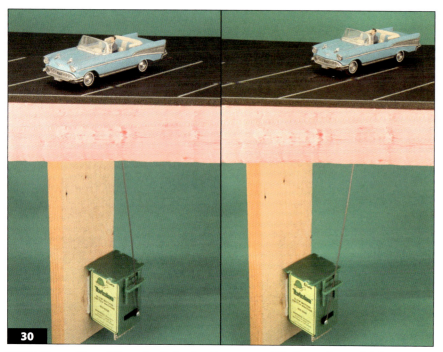

30

Notice the position of the extended rod as it moves to shift the car forward (left) and back (right).

Animating a vehicle

Everyone knows that action on a layout doesn't have to come only from the trains. Operating accessories add life to a railroad and enhance the fun quotient. Another surprise can come from the replication of a real-life occurrence on any city street. With a little imagination and some slow-motion switch machines, you can bring parts of your layout to life.

Photo **26** shows a busy city street corner. A fire truck passes by, a young family is out for a stroll, and a motorcycle policeman speeds off to some emergency. Like most model railroad scenes, this is essentially a still life, with one surprising exception. Notice the young man in his blue 1957 Chevrolet Bel Air convertible, backing out of an angled parking space. The little Chevy actually moves.

A few years ago I converted my layout to Atlas O track, leaving me with a large number of Tortoise slow-motion switch machines to gather dust in my spare parts box. It occurred to me that these useful devices could be used to add animation to otherwise static areas of my layout, **27**.

A Tortoise switch machine is a motorized device with a protruding shaft that moves laterally back and forth. A thin, springy metal rod attached to this shaft is supported by a fulcrum. When the switch machine is mounted beneath the layout table, the rod extends upward through the fulcrum and the layout table into the drawbar of a turnout. The machine operates by the rod moving the drawbar to throw the turnout. The fulcrum can be moved up or down to vary the amount of movement of the rod. The motion of the switch machine can also be used to animate any scene where lateral motion is desired, in this case backing a car out of an angled parking space.

Select a vehicle model with a hole in the bottom, such as a Matchbox Dinky Chevrolet convertible. Using a No. 11 blade in a hobby knife, cut a slot approximately 3½" long in the roadway, in the center of the parking space. The exact location of the slot will depend upon where the hole is located in the bottom of the car, **28**. The car should be all the way into the space when the hole is above one end of the slot and partially out into the road when the hole is above the opposite end.

The rod that comes with the switch machine is too short for this particular application, **29**. It should extend above the roadway just enough to reach into the hole in the bottom of the car (about ½" for this Matchbox Dinky model). Cut a new length of piano wire (available from hobby shops) about 12" long. This will allow lateral motion of about 3½", the length of the slot in the parking space. Bend one end of the wire to fit in the hole in the shaft, and hold it in place with the screw that comes with the machine.

Notice the position of the shaft and the rod, **30**. When the shaft moves in one direction, the rod pivots in the fulcrum to move in the opposite direction. When the switch machine's motor is operated, the shaft moves left, and the car backs slowly out of the parking space; reverse the switch, and the car pulls forward and parks.

Wiring the switch machine

There are several ways to wire the Tortoise switch machine. Since it contains a direct current (DC) motor, it cannot be operated by an alternating current (AC) transformer (standard type of power supply for three-rail O gauge trains) without modification. But it can be operated by any DC power pack, such as those that come with HO and N scale train sets, **31**. Connect the track power output of the power pack to the two outermost terminals on the switch machine. The other six are not used. The machine runs at a realistically slow speed at about 9 to 12 volts, and will operate in either direction, using the reverse mechanism of the power pack. If you use the accessory power output of a DC power pack rather than the track power output, you will not be able to reverse the direction of the switch machine motor unless you wire it through a double-pole double-throw (DPDT) toggle switch.

If you don't have a spare DC power pack, you can use any simple 9 to 12 volt charger, like those that come with portable CD or DVD players (one is shown in photo **31**). But you'll need a way to reverse the

Tortoise switch machines are designed to operate using direct current (DC). Use a plug-in wall charger or HO train set power pack to activate the animation.

flow of current to make the switch machine operate in both directions. Cut off the charger's small plug (the plug that inserts in the device to be charged), and connect the two wires to a miniature center-off DPDT toggle switch (available at electronics supply stores). There are six terminals on the back of the switch. Connect jumper wires between the outer four terminals, **32**. Connect the charger to the two middle terminals and the switch machine to two of the end terminals. The switch machine will operate in either direction, depending upon which way the toggle switch is thrown. (This wiring diagram also

works with the accessory power output of a DC power pack.)

Finally, you can use a Lionel, MTH, or other toy train transformer by converting the AC voltage to DC with a bridge rectifier (available at electronics supply stores). Use transformer accessory terminals that provide approximately 9 to 12 volts. Connect the accessory terminals to the AC terminals of the rectifier, and connect the DC terminals to the middle terminals of the toggle switch, **33**.

In the next chapter, we'll use foam core illustration board to create a centerpiece for your layout, a special display that gives it a unique identity.

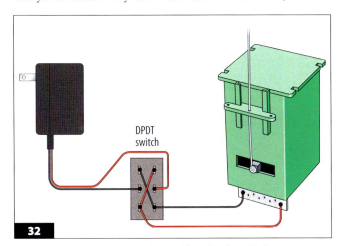

To wire a Tortoise switch machine with a plug-in wall charger, connect jumper wires between the outer terminals, the charger to the middle terminals, and the switch machine to the end terminals.

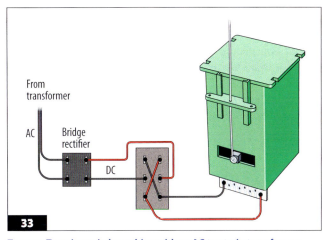

To use a Tortoise switch machine with an AC toy train transformer, connect accessory terminals to AC terminals on a bridge rectifier and connect the DC terminals to the middle terminals of the toggle switch.

CHAPTER EIGHT

Creating a layout centerpiece

Modern technology meets 1950s Americana in this twilight drive-in movie scene.

Every layout should have a centerpiece, something unusual that visitors will find especially interesting. While many model railroads rely upon readily available commercial items to stimulate interest, such as the operating accessories made by Lionel, MTH, and others, it's the unexpected features you create yourself that will make your railroad memorable. Here's an idea for one such display—a miniature drive-in theater right out of the 1950s, using today's technology, **1**.

To build a DVD drive-in, first cut a screen-width slot into a piece of foam core board. Use the slot to guide a cut in the foam tabletop.

Test that the screen and additional components of the DVD player fit through the slot and function properly.

Use a sharp hobby knife to cut black foam core board into the pieces needed to build an enclosure for the DVD player.

After assembling the enclosure, paint a gray strip along the base to simulate a concrete foundation.

A portable DVD player or tablet with a 7" or 8" screen is the perfect size to re-create a drive-in for an O gauge layout. It looks good in daylight and is especially effective when the room lights are dimmed to suggest a twilight showing. All you need to make the scene authentic are several simple structures built from foam core illustration board, some model cars, and a few small details.

Choose a location for the theater where the screen will be clearly visible. Cut out an illustration board to fit the area as described in previous chapters.

Measure the base of the DVD player and cut a slot in the board, **2**. Using a thin-bladed kitchen knife, also cut a hole in the rigid foam table top the same size as the slot. (If you have a plywood table, you will need a keyhole saw for this step.) The DVD player will be inserted through the holes and placed upright to represent the drive-in screen. (Portable tablets will fit a little differently in the hole.)

Be sure to buy a DVD player that opens to a full 180 degrees. The base of the player should fit snugly when inserted in the slot, **3**. Slide it in until

the lower part of the screen portion lies on top of the illustration board, while the rest of the mechanism is suspended below the table. It is important to be able to remove the player from the slot in order to turn the unit on and off and to change the movie disks.

Encasing the player

You will need an enclosure to disguise the true nature of the player. It's easy to build with foam core illustration board. Measure the player and construct a shallow box to fit over the screen. It should be just large enough so that the

Use brick paper to laminate the walls of the enclosure. Trim the paper to fit between the roof and the painted foundation.

Word processing applications are handy tools for creating custom signs for nearly any layout structure.

Cut strips of basswood or balsa to make the frame used to hold the enclosure in place atop the layout.

Paint these wood strips gray to match the concrete foundation.

case of the unit will be hidden, while the entire screen remains visible. You will need to cut a back wall slightly larger than the case, two side walls, and a top, **4**.

Paint a gray strip around the bottom of the box to simulate a concrete foundation, **5**. For an all-concrete enclosure, you could paint it completely gray, but it will look more realistic if you cover it with brick paper.

You can buy brick paper in a variety of colors and patterns from hobby shops and online suppliers such as Scenic Express. Cut the paper to fit between the top and the painted foun-dation area, **6**. It should be wide enough to extend all the way around the front. Crease the paper to make a crisp fold at the corners by scoring it lightly on the back with a scissors blade.

Rubber cement is an ideal adhe-sive for fastening paper to illustration board. Put a thin coat on both the enclosure and the back of the paper, and let it dry until tacky. Wrap the paper around the enclosure and press it down firmly. The cement will bond instantly, so be sure to line it up care-fully first.

You might want to make a paper sign to identify the name of your theater, **7**. I used a word processing program and printed it in a blue italic font. To mount the sign, cut a small strip of illustration board and glue it across the front of the enclosure.

Slide the enclosure down over the DVD screen. Cut strips of basswood or balsa to make a framework to keep the enclosure in place, **8**. Glue the strips to the illustration board. Be careful not to get any glue on the enclosure, as you must be able to lift it off whenever you want access to the DVD player. Paint the wood strips gray to match the foundation area of the enclosure, **9**.

10

This photo shows the enclosed structure lifted off to expose the DVD player's screen positioned above the layout where the components fit into the slot.

Photo **10** shows the enclosure lifted off to expose the DVD player. To turn the unit on or off or to change the disk, you simply lift out the player, do whatever is necessary, and reinsert it in the slot. Then slip the enclosure over it again, fitting it in between the wooden strips around the base.

Some drive-in theaters still exist (including one in Waterville, Nova Scotia, not far from our home). Many drive-in theaters were built in grassy fields, with narrow dirt or gravel roadways. Use a pencil to outline these areas on the illustration board, **11**. Block out parking places large enough to accommodate your model cars. Sprinkle the landscape material over wet paint and vacuum up the excess when it has dried. Don't forget to put in strips of dirt to show where the tires of the cars wear away the grass.

11

Use a pencil to sketch a parking lot onto a foam core board. Paint both sides of the board and add turf material to the top side.

Adding extra details will fill out the scene. Be sure to add seated figures in the vehicles and speakers to broadcast the movie's sound. Other details can include flowers and fences along the lot perimeter.

Add extra details to the scene, such as a fence in front of the screen and flower beds. To provide an audience, you can obtain human figures that are especially made to fit inside your model cars from your local hobby shop, **12**.

One important detail should not be left out—speaker poles for the movie sound system. It was common practice to locate one pole with two speakers between each pair of cars, located next to the front seat. Depending upon which side of the pole you parked on, the speaker would be hung on either the driver's side window or the passenger's. You can make very simple poles and speakers from finishing nails and small rectangles of balsa wood painted black.

Many drive-in theaters had a playground to keep the kids occupied until show time, **13**. Submerge it into the scenery as described in Chapter 7. You can make a combination ticket booth and refreshment counter from illustration board or adapt one of Lionel's amusement park booths as shown, with the addition of a sign produced with a word processing program.

To complete the scene, you will need a projection booth, **14**, which is a simple rectangular box made from illustration board and covered with brick paper. Provide two holes for the projectors (put a small grain-of-wheat light bulb inside) and two peepholes for the operators to keep track of the screen (and the audience). Don't forget to put a door in one side of the building.

The sign next to the entrance is an animated chase light made by Light Works USA and sold by Scenic Express. You can mount it on another illustration board structure, such as this half wall covered with brick paper. Don't forget to provide a few lampposts, so the customers will be able to see when driving home after the movie. (The lampposts in my drive-in were made by American Flyer prior to World War II.)

Whenever you invite guests in to see your railroad, I suggest that you dim the lights and turn on the DVD player before they enter the room, **15**. It will probably be the one thing they remember best about their visit. And you might also want to pop in a favorite movie whenever you work on the layout.

This brings us to the end of our journey. As you work on your layout, experiment with different scenery methods and have fun.

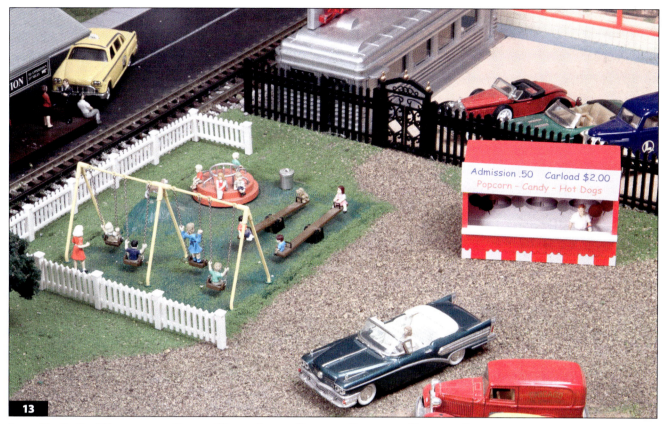

Every drive-in should have a concession stand for moviegoers. You can make one out of foam core illustration board or adapt a Lionel amusement park booth as I did. Many drive-in theaters also had playgrounds, such as this Lionel accessory, to keep children amused.

A projection booth at the rear of the property completes the Galaxy Drive-in. The booth is a simple rectangle made of foam core board covered with simulated brick paper.

15

By adding a centerpiece to your layout, such as the Galaxy Drive-in, you provide visitors with a more memorable experience.

About the author

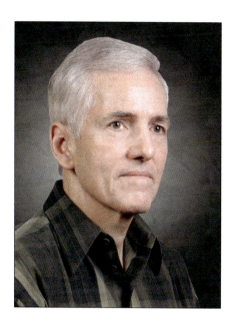

Peter Riddle is a lifelong toy train enthusiast—he received his first Lionel set at age five. After 44 years in the teaching profession, 36 of them as Professor of Music at Acadia University in Wolfville, Nova Scotia, he is currently pursuing a second career as an author. *Scenery Techniques for Toy Trains* is his 13th book about model railroading, and he is a regular contributor to *Classic Toy Trains* magazine. His wife Gay, who shares his interest in the hobby, assists him with these manuscripts.

Peter has also published a text book on the subject of American musical theatre, eight novels, two novelettes for young readers, and, in collaboration with illustrator Shelley Hustins, a children's book for Christmas. He and Gay have two children and three grandchildren.

Acknowledgments

The author gratefully acknowledges the assistance and expertise provided by the helpful staff at Scenic Express (www.scenicexpress.com).

The track products used in constructing the layouts that appear in this book were provided by Atlas O (www.atlaso.com), Ross Custom Switches (www,rossswitches.com), and GarGraves Trackage Corporation (www.gargraves.com).

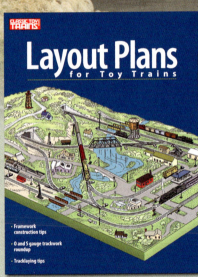
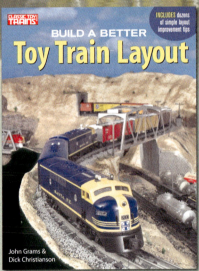
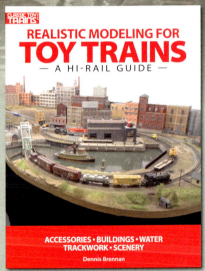